Hope

The following Oswald Chambers books are available
from Discovery House Publishers:

Hope _A Holy Promise_

Oswald Chambers

Compiled and Edited by
JULIE ACKERMAN LINK

DISCOVERY HOUSE
PUBLISHERS®

Hope: A Holy Promise
© 2009 by Oswald Chambers Publications Association
Limited. All rights reserved.

Discovery House Publishers is affiliated with RBC
Ministries, Grand Rapids, Michigan.

Discovery House books are distributed to the trade
exclusively by Barbour Publishing, Inc., Uhrichsville, Ohio.

All Scripture quotations are from the New King James
Version. Copyright © 1979, 1980, 1982 by Thomas
Nelson, Inc., Publishers.

Questions by Julie Ackerman Link

Library of Congress Cataloging-in-Publication Data
Available on request.

ISBN: 978-1-57293-308-8

Printed in the United States of America
09 10 11 12 13 14 15 16 / DPI / 10 9 8 7 6 5 4 3 2 1

Contents

Introduction

"For the Christian, hope is a noun," says my friend Doug Fagerstrom. When I heard him say this, we were in the Judean wilderness, walking along the treacherous ancient road between Jerusalem and Jericho, overlooking the valley of the shadow, which many believe is the location that inspired David's twenty-third psalm. The place itself offers little reason for hope. The landscape is bleak, barren, and perilously steep. To survive in such a place requires hope in something other than natural resources, for nature's provisions are unseen and unreliable. Finding green grass and still water requires a miracle, not just skill.

When David wrote, "Even though I walk through the valley of the shadow of death, I will fear no evil," he was in a place where evil was an ever-present reality. So he wasn't expressing hope that God would abolish evil so that he could pass through safely; he was saying that the presence of God gave him the confidence to pass through evil places without fear of being destroyed.

In other psalms, David said that his hope was in the Lord. Hope comes not from our surroundings, our circumstances, or our experiences. Hope comes from the Lord. As maker of heaven and earth, He alone can promise hope and keep the promise.

Scripture indicates that hope is indeed more than an action or an emotion. Hope is something that we *have*, not simply something that we *do*, as in wishing for something we want. Nor is it something that we *feel*, as in feeling optimistic, nor a state of mind, as in thinking positively.

Oswald Chambers has much to say about having hope, and he uses several words to convey the concept, as does Scripture—words such as trust, confidence, and certainty. Our hope is grounded in the *trustworthiness* of God. We can have *confidence* in that hope because the Holy Spirit confides to us the mysteries of God. And our hope is made *certain* by Christ and His resurrection. As Chambers says,

> Mathematics is the rule of reason and common sense, but . . . hope is the rule of the spiritual. We are gloriously uncertain of the next step, but we are certain of God.

Circumstances may cause us to think that God is losing the battle against evil, but Christ's death and resurrection give us hope that God's promise to defeat evil is even now being realized through His work in us. "Jesus Christ's hope is that the human race will be as He is himself," says Chambers, "perfectly at one with God." This is the hope that we *have*, the glorious hope of Christ in us.

—Julie Ackerman Link

In Doubt

Hope *in* GOD

GOD'S SEED WILL always bring forth fruit if it is put in the right conditions. Man cannot order the seasons or make the seed to grow (cf. Jeremiah 33:20); and we are powerless to make saints. Our duty is to put the seed into the right place and leave the rest to God. It would be foolish for a farmer to sow his seed and tell his servants to watch it; he must sow his seed in the right place and then trust in God and Nature, and by and by he will reap his harvest. So all we can do is to sow the seed of the Word of God in the hearts of the hearers.[SHL]

Reflection Questions

In what ways do I try to do God's work? Or expect others to do it? If I truly place all my hope in God, what difference will this make in the priorities I set and the work I do?

A LITTLE CHILD is certain of its parents, but uncertain about everything else, therefore it lives a perfectly delightful healthy life.[LG]

"IF YOU OBEY Jesus you will have a life of joy and delight." Well, it is not true. Jesus said to the disciples, "Let us go to the other side of the lake," and they were plunged into the biggest storm they had ever known. You say, "If I had not obeyed Jesus I should not have got into this complication." Exactly. The temptation is to say, "God could never have told me to go there, if He had done so this would not have happened." We discover then whether we are going to trust God's integrity or listen to our own expressed skepticism.[HSGM]

Reflection Questions

When things go badly, do I see it as an indication that I have been mistaken about God's leading or about God's love? Am I prepared to accept that perhaps neither is true? What better explanation is there?

"THE SACRIFICES OF God are a broken spirit" (Psalm 51:17)—that of a spirit God has made glad by a great forgiveness. The sign of this kind of broken heart is that the saint is untroubled by storms, and undismayed by bereavement because he is confident in God.[NJ]

A PARABLE IS an earthly story which does not explain itself. Every one of us has an earthly story, and the explanation of it is not to be found in its own expression, but only in the domain of the Designer of life. Job says that the explanation his friends give of his earthly story is hopeless, they are nowhere near understanding it; God alone is the Source from whence will come the explanation of all he is going through.[BFB]

Reflection Questions

What do my feelings of hopelessness tell me about my knowledge of God? Do the opinions of my friends add to my hope in God or subtract from it? What does my concept of prosperity tell me about my hope in God?

A MAN'S IDEA of prosperity is according to where his hopes are founded—on God or on a hearsay God; on the living God, or on ideas of God. It is in the way alone with God that the soul says with Job, "I have heard of you . . . but now my eye sees you" (42:5).[CD]

A WISE MAN who has built his life in confidence in God will appear a fool when he is among people who are sleek and cunning. The wisdom of God is arrant stupidity to the wisdom of the world, until all of a sudden God makes the wisdom of the world foolish (1 Corinthians 1:23–25). If you stand true to your faith in God, there will be situations in which you will come across extortioners, cunning, crafty people, who use their wits instead of worshipping God, and you will appear a fool. Are you prepared to appear a fool for Christ's sake?[SHH]

Reflection Questions

In what ways does my hope in God make me appear foolish to my friends and colleagues? When I am vindicated for remaining true to my hope in God, how will I show grace to those whose craftiness has failed them?

ALONE WITH GOD! All hope and all aspiration springs from that source, and consequently all prosperity is measured from that source, and prosperity that springs from any other source is looked upon as disastrous.[CD]

ALL CERTAINTY BRINGS death to something. When we have a certain belief, we kill God in our lives, because we do not believe Him, we believe our beliefs about Him and do what Job's friends did—bring God and human life to the standard of our beliefs and not to the standard of God. The helplessness of professional religion is that there is no room for surprise, we tie God up in His laws and in denominational doctrines and orders of services, consequently we do not see God at all.[LG]

Reflection Questions

What false sense of confidence am I willing to put to death so that my confidence in God can be fully alive? In what ways do I place my hope in religious practices rather than in the power of the resurrected Christ?

WHEREVER WE TRUST in goodness or nobility instead of in God, we suddenly find ourselves in a howling waste wilderness. The attitude of a godly life is to put no confidence in anything or anyone but God.[NJ]

In Doubt: Hope *in* GOD

IN THE ORDINARY everyday things of life—eating and drinking, cleaning your boots, writing an essay—is it slovenly? is it careless and indifferent? does self-indulgence come in? That little pinhole exhibits the dry rot that runs all through everything you do, and when you trust God in a shabby, defective way—"I will have faith in God about this matter, but not about that"—then you don't trust God at all. If we will examine ourselves in the light of the things that can be seen we will realize that that is how God sees us all through.[GW]

Reflection Questions

Do I hope in God for "little" things or just "big" things? Do I rely on God for everything or just things that bewilder me? How does hope manifest itself in my ordinary, everyday life?

IT IS EASIER to rely on God in big things than in little things. There is an enormous power in little things to distract our attention from God; that is why our Lord said that "the cares of this world," "the lusts of other things," would choke the word and make it unfruitful.[HG]

ALONE WITH GOD! It is there that what is hid with God is made known—God's ideals, God's hopes, God's doings. The intense individual responsibility of walking among men from the standpoint of being alone with the real God, is never guessed until we do stand alone with God. It is a hidden thing, so hidden that it seems not only untenable but a wild quixotic thing to do, and so it would be if God were not known to be real.[CD]

Reflection Questions

What scares me about being alone with God? What am I hiding that I think God doesn't see? What do I think I need that I fear God won't give me? What do I hope for that God won't provide?

BEWARE OF TRUSTING in your trust and see that you trust in the Lord, and you will never know you trust Him because you are taken up into His certainty.[NKW]

WHEN GOD GIVES a vision and darkness follows, wait; God will bring you into accordance with the vision He has given if you will wait His time. We try to do away with the supernatural in God's undertakings. Never try and help God fulfill His word. There are some things we cannot do, and that is one of them.[NKW]

Reflection Questions

Is my hope strong enough to wait on God or must I always jump in to "help" Him? Do I have enough hope in God to not do anything even though it seems as if something must be done?

CERTAINTY OF GOD means uncertainty in life; while certainty in belief makes us uncertain of God. Certainty is the mark of the common-sense life; gracious uncertainty is the mark of the spiritual life, and they must both go together.[LG]

DARKNESS IS NOT synonymous with sin; if there is darkness spiritually it is much more likely to be the shade of God's hand than darkness on account of sin; it may be the threshold of a new revelation coming through a big break in personal experience. Before the dawn there is desolation; but wait, the dawn will merge into glorious day.[HSGM]

Reflection Questions

Do I lose hope when darkness closes in? Do I use darkness as an opportunity to rest and trust, or do I see darkness as a reason not to rest or trust? In what ways do I equate darkness with sinfulness?

WHEN GOD PUTS the dark of "nothing" into your experience, it is the most positive something He can give you. Remain in the center of nothing, and say "thank you" for nothing. It is a very great lesson, which few of us learn, that when God gives us nothing it is because we are inside Him, and by determining to do something we put ourselves outside Him.[NKW]

In Doubt: Hope *in* GOD

NEVER TRY TO anticipate the actual fulfillment of a vision; you transact some business spiritually with God on your mount of transfiguration and by faith see clearly a vision of His purpose, and immediately afterwards there is nothing but blank darkness. You trust in the Lord, but you walk in darkness; the temptation is to work up enthusiasm, you have to stay on God and wait (Isaiah 50:10–11). If darkness turns to spiritual doldrums, you are to blame.NKW

Reflection Questions

In what way has the gloom of circumstances outside myself caused gloom in my inner self? What flame am I tempted to light to bring brightness to my life that might result in a raging fire with the potential to destroy all that God is building?

GOD GRANT WE may accept His clouds and mysteries, and be led into His inner secrets by obedient trust.PH

IF A MAN will resign himself in implicit trust to the Lord Jesus, he will find that He leads the wayfaring soul into the green pastures and beside the still waters, so that even when he goes through the dark valley of the shadow of some staggering episode, he will fear no evil. Nothing in life or death, time or eternity, can stagger that soul from the certainty of the Way for one moment.[PH]

Reflection Questions

Are there green pastures under my feet that I can't see because of darkness? Is there a source of still water that I've not found because I'm afraid to move in the dark? What causes me to lose hope that God will lead me safely to the place He wants me to be?

THERE ARE THINGS God tells us to do without any light or illumination other than just the word of His command, and if we do not obey, it is because we are independently strong enough to wriggle out of obeying. All God's commands are enablings; therefore, it is a crime to be weak in His strength.[NKW]

IF I LET the sorrow of a bereaved home weigh on me, instantly my faith in God is gone; I am so overcome with sympathy that my prayer is nothing more than a wail of sympathy before God. The influence of my mind on another, whether I speak or not, is so subtle that the prince of this world will use it to prevent my getting hold of God; whereas if I remain confident in God I lift the weight off lives in a way I shall never realize till I stand before Him. We have to pray that the enemy shall not make God's children slander Him by worry and anxiety. We are to hold off the exactings of Satan, not add to them.GW

Reflection Questions

How does my worry and anxiety slander God?
How does hope exalt Him?

EVERY TIME GOD presents us with a problem, He gives us something to match it in our own heart, and if we will let His power work there, we shall go forth with unshakeable confidence in what He can do. Once we know that God can do what Jesus Christ said He could, we can never be put in the place where we will be discouraged.SSIY

IF YOUR HOPES are being disappointed just now it means that they are being purified. There is nothing noble the human mind has ever hoped for or dreamed of that will not be fulfilled. Don't jump to conclusions too quickly; many things lie unsolved, and the biggest test of all is that God looks as if He were totally indifferent. Remain spiritually tenacious.[GW]

Reflection Questions

What wrong conclusions about God cause me to lose hope? What circumstances cause me to think of God as indifferent? Why does the hope of Redemption require us to go through difficult circumstances?

IN THE BIBLE you never find the note of the pessimist. In the midst of the most crushing conditions there is always an extraordinary hopefulness and profound joy, because God is at the heart. The effective working of Redemption in our experience makes us leap for joy in the midst of things in which other people see nothing but disastrous calamity.[HG]

In Doubt: Hope *in* GOD

IN A SERMON some years ago, Father Frere said, "Have you ever had to do something to a pet dog in order to get it well, something which hurt it very much—pulled a thorn out of its foot, or washed out a wound, or anything of that sort? If so, you will remember the expression of dumb eloquence in the eyes of the dog as he looked at you; what you were doing hurt him tremendously and yet there seemed to speak from his eyes such a trust of you as if he would say, 'I don't in the least understand what you are doing, what you are doing hurts, but go on with it.'"

That is an apt illustration of suffering "according to the will of God."[CD]

Reflection Questions

What is God doing that defies understanding? What do I hope to gain by resisting? What can I hope to gain by trusting?

SOMETIMES WE HAVE to look up mutely to God and say, "I don't understand it at all, but go on with what You are doing." That marks a real stage of learning to trust in God. Spiritual experience has begun; suffering has already deepened the soul.[CD]

23

JESUS CHRIST'S THOUGHT about man is that he is lost, and that He is the only One who can find him. Salvation means that if a man will turn—and every man has the power to turn, if it is only a look towards the Cross, he has the power for that—if a man will but turn, he will find that Jesus is able to deliver him not only from the snare of the wrong disposition within him, but from the power of evil and wrong outside him. As soon as a man turns, God finds him. The Cross of Christ spells hope for the most despairing sinner on the face of the earth.[CHI]

Reflection Questions

Is my hope in God strong enough to cause me to turn away from sin? Why or why not? What causes me to have more hope in going my own way than God's way?

GOD IS RULING and reigning, and His character is holy.[SHH]

In Doubt: Hope *in* GOD

THE SUFFERING OF Job is accounted for by the fact that God and Satan had made a battleground of his life. Satan has declared that Job does not love God for himself, but only for His blessings, and now everything in the way of shelter and comradeship and sympathy has been completely stripped from Job, and he sees that God must have allowed it. This is the deepest line Job has come to as yet, but he still clings to it that God is honorable. This is supreme despair, along with extraordinary confidence in God who meantime looks like a moloch.[HG]

Reflection Questions

Do I love God for himself or for His blessings? What happens to my confidence in God when He withholds blessing?

JOB BELIEVED THAT God prospered and blessed the upright man who trusted in Him, and that the man who was not upright was not prospered. Then came calamity after calamity. Everything Job believed about God was contradicted, and his creed went to the winds.[BFB]

Satan NOT ONLY slanders God to us, but accuses us to God. It is as if he looked down and pointed out a handful of people and insinuated to God, "Now, that woman is a perfect disgrace to You, she has only one spark of grace among all the fibers of her life; I advise You to stamp out that spark." What is the revelation? "He will raise it to a flame." Or, he points out a man and says, "That man is a disgrace to You, he is a 'bruised reed,' I wonder You build any hope on him whatever, he is a hindrance and an upset to You, break him!" But no, the Lord will bind him up and make him into a wonderful instrument.[BP]

Reflection Questions

Have I lost hope because I consider myself a disgrace to God? How would my hope be revitalized if I considered instead that God has hope for me?

The OLD REEDS were used to make wonderful musical instruments, and instead of crushing out the life that is bruised and wrong, God heals it and discourses sweet music through it.[BP]

In Doubt: Hope *in* GOD

THE BOOKS OF Wisdom are strong on facing facts, and yet there is no touch of despair underneath. In all other books which face things as they are, there is tremendous pessimism and abject despair, no hope whatever; but in Solomon's writings, while he maintains a ruggedness and an intensity and an unswerving truthfulness to facts, there is an extraordinary hopefulness running all through, and that without getting sentimental and falling back on the kindness of God.[SHH]

Reflection Questions

What are the worst facts I have to face? How do these "facts" affect my faith? How does hope transcend horrible circumstances?

THE MINOR PROPHETS state appalling facts, enough to knock hope out of any man, but the Hebrew writers never seem to despair however bad the facts may be, there is always the indefinable certainty that there is something to hope about.[SHH]

SIN, SUFFERING, AND sanctification are not problems of the mind, but facts of life—mysteries that awaken all other mysteries until the heart rests in God. Oh, the unspeakable joy of knowing that God reigns! that He is our Father, and that the clouds are but "the dust of His feet"! Religious life is based and built up and matured on primal implicit trust, transfigured by Love.^{CD}

Reflection Questions

What keeps me from resting in God? How does love nourish hope? What might happen if I thought more about my relationship with God and less about achieving certain results?

WHEN I GET my eyes off Him I begin to get weary. I am kept from wasting in the way only as I abide under the shadow of the Almighty and stake my all in confidence in God. I have nothing to do with the results, but only with maintaining my relationship to Him.^{PH}

THE DISCIPLES HAD given up everything for Jesus; they had followed Him for three years; Peter and the other disciples think this is the time when He will introduce His kingdom; instead, the whole thing ends in humiliating insignificance. Peter never dreamed he was going to see Jesus Christ give himself up meekly to the power of the world, and he was broken-hearted and "followed Him afar off." To call Peter a coward for following Jesus afar off is an indication of how we talk without thinking. Peter and all the disciples were broken-hearted, everything they had hoped for with regard to Jesus Christ had failed, and now their worst fears were realized.[HSGM]

Reflection Questions

What circumstances cause me to think that God is losing the battle against evil? What does Christ's death and resurrection tell me about God's power over evil? What fear do I have that isn't overcome by the hope of resurrection?

MANY A CHRISTIAN since Peter has suffered complete heartbreak, not because he fears anything personally, but because it looks as if his Lord is being worsted.[HSGM]

THERE IS NO reasonable hope for countless lives, and it is shallow nonsense to tell them to "cheer up." Life to them is a hell of darkness of the most appalling order. The one who preaches at such a time is an impertinence, but the one who says "I don't know why you are going through this, it is black and desperate, but I will wait with you," is an unspeakable benediction and sustaining. Job has no one to do this for him, his one-time friends simply add to his bitterness.[BFB]

Reflection Questions

Are my conversations more likely to inspire hope or hopelessness? In what ways can I offer hope to someone in despair?

THE DECREES OF despair lie underneath everything a man does when once he rules out his relationship to God and takes rationalism as the basis of life. Solomon sums up the whole matter—unless a man is rightly related in confidence to God, everything he tries to do will end in despair.[SHH]

WE ALL EXPERIENCE the weariness that comes from wrongdoing, but there is also a weariness that comes in well-doing, when everything becomes listless. It has no business to be though—it is a sickness of the soul. What is the cure? The cure is that of a right vision. Every man has the power to slay his own weariness, not by "bucking up" as you do physically, but by suddenly looking at things from a different standpoint.[PH]

Reflection Questions

Is my weariness caused by wrongdoing or welldoing? How are they related? What wrong view of the world causes both? What new attitude or viewpoint do I need so that I can see life from a better perspective?

IT IS A tremendous thing to know that God reigns and rules and rejoices, and that His joy is our strength. The confidence of a Christian is that God is the Father of lights who remains unaffected by darkness.[PH]

JOB REFUSES TO allow his religious beliefs to blind him to what he sees, and he refuses to tell a lie either for the honor of God or for his own comfort. When suffering and perplexity bring us in touch with the problems at the heart of life, we will probably do one of two things—either tell a lie for the honor of God and say, "I must be much worse than I thought I was," or else accept a form of belief which does away with thinking. Most of us take our salvation much too cheaply. There is no hope for Job, and no hope for anyone on the face of the earth, unless God does something for him.[BFB]

Reflection Questions

What circumstances cause me to think wrongly about myself or God? What happens to my theology if I can't judge by my circumstances?

GOD EXPECTS HIS children to be so confident in Him that in a crisis they are the ones upon whom He can rely. God expects of us the one thing that glorifies Him—and that is to remain absolutely confident in Him, remembering what He has said beforehand, and sure that His purposes will be fulfilled.[PH]

In Doubt: Hope *in* GOD

THERE ARE PEOPLE today who are going through an onslaught of destruction that paralyzes all our platitudes and preaching; the only thing that will bring relief is the consolations of Christ. It is a good thing to feel our own powerlessness in the face of destruction; it makes us know how much we depend upon God. Not every cloud has a silver lining; there are some clouds that are black all through. Even so, we go through sorrow not callously, but with an extraordinary sense of hopefulness.[BFB]

Reflection Questions

Why is it good to feel powerless? Why then do I try so hard to feel strong? How can I keep from placing my hope in my own strength?

IF I AM spiritual what I have to prove in a crisis is that God is sufficient to guide me in His own way; if I trust my wits it is all the god I have got, and God will hold me responsible for my fanaticism and delusion.[NE]

WHEN WE ARE in fear, we can do nothing less than pray to God, but our Lord has the right to expect of those who name His Name and have His nature in them an understanding confidence in Him. Instead of that, when we are at our wits' end we go back to the elementary prayers of those who do not know Him, and prove that we have not the slightest atom of confidence in Him and in His government of the world.[PH]

Reflection Questions

Do I have more hope in the promise of God to establish His government or in the promise of politicians? How do my prayers reveal lack of faith? What does fear tell God about my confidence in Him?

OUR LORD REBUKED the disciples for fearing when apparently they had good reason for being alarmed. The problem is—if Jesus Christ is the Son of God, what are they alarmed about? If Jesus Christ is God, where is my trust in Him? If He is not God, why am I so foolish as to pretend to worship Him?[HSGM]

NOTHING IS SO disastrously enervating as disillusionment. We much prefer our fictions and fairy stories about ourselves, to the stern realization of what we really are in God's sight. In spiritual life disillusionment generally comes in relation to other people. For Ezekiel, the disillusionment came in connection with national life and in relation to God: the people began to realize that God is not what they had vainly hoped He was.[NE]

Reflection Questions
Do I have hope in who God is or in who I want Him to be? What illusions do I prefer over reality?

THE WAY WE act when we come up against things proves whether we have been disillusioned or not; do we trust in our wits or do we worship God? If we trust in our wits, God will have to repeat the same lesson until we learn it. Whenever our faith is not in God, and in Him alone, there is still an illusion somewhere.[PH]

THERE ARE TIMES in sorrow when we are disillusioned, our eyes are opened, and we see people in their true relationships, and often we get completely disheartened and feel we won't trust anyone any more. But when we are trusting our Lord Jesus Christ, this kind of light affliction leaves us with a true discernment, we are not deceived, we see men and women in their right relationship, and light comes all through. Whatever happens, our relationship to Jesus Christ works through it. We have to learn to take up pain and weave it into the fabric of our lives.[PH]

Reflection Questions
How does my trust in other people interfere with my trust in God? What part does pain play in my testimony?

I THINK WE are losing sight of the real meaning of testimony; it is not for the sake of others, but for our own sake. It makes us know we have no one to rely on but God.[SHL]

IN JOB'S CASE there was every element to make him conceive of God as an unkind Friend, an unnatural Father, and an unjust Judge; but through everything, Job stuck to his belief in the character of God. Job lost his hereditary creed, which was that God blessed and prospered physically and materially the man who trusted in Him, but his words, "though He slay me, yet will I trust in Him," prove how tenaciously he clung to God.[CD]

Reflection Questions

How does God's willingness to "appear" unkind and unloving affect my hope? What small things erode my hope?

MANY THINGS WILL destroy confidence; as in the case of Jacob, cunning and sin will do it, or cowardice; but in every experience of misgiving there is an element that is difficult to define, and the shallow element is the most difficult. "I can't understand why I have no confidence in God"; the reason may be a matter of digestion, not enough fresh air, or sleep, too much tea—something slight. It is the small things that put us wrong much more quickly than the big things.[OPG]

NO MATTER WHAT revelations God has made to you, there will be destitution so far as the physical apprehension of things is concerned—God gives you a revelation that He will provide, then He provides nothing and you begin to realize that there is a famine, of food, or of clothes, or money, and your commonsense says, "Abandon your faith in God." Do it at your peril. Watch where destitution comes; if it comes on the heels of a time of quiet confidence in God, then thank Him for it.^{OPG}

Reflection Questions

What happens to my hope when God doesn't give me what I want? Where do I go for help when I don't get what I want from God?

FAITH IS NOT a bargain with God—I will trust You if You give me money, but not if You don't. We have to trust in God whether He sends us money or not, whether He gives us health or not. We must have faith in God, not in His gifts. Let us walk before God and be perfect, you in your circumstances and I in mine.^{NKW}

In Doubt: Hope *in* GOD

FAITH IN GOD is a terrific venture in the dark. We have to believe that God is love in spite of all that contradicts it. Every soul represents some kind of battlefield. The great point for the Christian is to remain perfectly confident in God. Paul says that when the sons of God are manifested, and everything is in a right relationship with God and expressed in devotion to Jesus Christ, all the wildness and contradiction in Nature and in nations will cease, and the Love of God will be the great Reality.[LG]

Reflection Questions

What is the battlefield of my soul today? How will I sustain my belief that God is love? Where can I look to see the love of God made real?

IT IS BECAUSE people live in the things they possess instead of in their relationship to God, that God at times seems to be cruel. There are a thousand and one interests that God's providential hand has to brush aside as hopelessly irrelevant to His purpose.[SSIY]

FAITH IS OUR personal confidence in a Being Whose character we know, but Whose ways we cannot trace by common sense. Faith is the practical out-working in our life of implicit, determined confidence in God. Common sense is mathematical; faith is not mathematical, faith works on illogical lines. Jesus Christ places the strongest emphasis on faith, and especially on the faith that has been tried.SSM

Reflection Questions

In what ways do I expect faith to work like a mathematical equation? In what ways do my interests and possessions keep me from being passionate about what is important to God?

EVERY CONFIDENCE, EVERY love, every devotion that is not based on a personal relationship to God will be reprobate, not only in the experience of the individual, but in the history of the world. God will demonstrate to us in His patient way that if we are building on anything less than Jesus Christ it will prove useless, because we have banked on the wrong thing (see 1 Cor. 3:10–15; 9:27).NJ

In Doubt: Hope *in* GOD

THE MAN OF faith hangs on to the fact that He is a God of honor. Fatalism means "my number's up," I have to bow to the power whether I like it or not; I do not know the character of the power, but it is greater than I am and I must submit. But we do know the character of God, although we do not know why His providential will should be as it is. The only thing to do in the present condition of things is to remain true to God, and God will not only see us through but will see the whole thing out to a perfect explanation.[SHH]

Reflection Questions
What hope do I find in the holy character of God? What does holiness have to do with hope? How does pain affect my hope?

PAIN WORKS FOR us an eternal hope. We have all had the experience that it is only in the days of affliction that our true interests are furthered.[PH]

A CHRISTIAN IS one who can live in the midst of the trouble and turmoil with the glory of God indwelling him, while he steadfastly looks not at the things which are seen, but at the things which are not seen. We have to learn to think only of things which are seen as a glorious chance of enabling us to concentrate on the things which are not seen. Then let the troubles and difficulties work as they may on the outside, we are confident that they are working out a grander weight of glory in the heavenlies.[LG]

Reflection Questions

How does the glory of God within me give me hope that I will never get lost in the black nothingness of the world outside of me?

IT IS NONSENSE to imagine that God expects me to discern all that is clear to His own mind. All He asks of me is to maintain perfect confidence in himself. Faith springs from the indwelling of the life of God in me.[OPG]

A DEAR LITTLE friend of mine, not four years old, facing some big difficulty to her little heart, with a very wise shake of her head, said, "I'll go and tell my papa." Presently she came back, this time strutting with pride, "Now, my papa's coming!" Presently her papa came, she clasped her little hands, screamed with delight, and danced round about him, unspeakably confident in her papa. Child of God, does something face you that terrifies your heart? Say, "I'll tell my Father." Then come back "boasting" in the Lord, "Now my Father's coming." And when He comes, you too will clasp your hands in rapture, your mouth will be filled with laughter, and you will be like one that dreams, when your Father comes.[CD]

Reflection Questions

If my earthly father was unreliable, how can I learn to have hope in my heavenly Father? What keeps me from surrendering my imperfect childhood to God?

OUR CONFIDENCE IS to be based on the fact that we give up being impressive individuals and give God the opportunity of dealing with men.[DI]

FROM THIS PRESENT order of things we infer an unseen power making for disintegration and destruction, yet in every human heart there lurks an implicit hope of a different order. These hopes ever fade and fall, and the vision tarries so long that hearts grow sick and embittered, and all seems to end in a poet's song, or a lover's passionate extravagance, or a dreamer's dream. But to the soul alone with God the secret is known and made real, and already a Paradise has begin that presages a grander and a greater blessedness than has entered into the heart of man to imagine.[CD]

---

*R*eflection *Q*uestions

What failed hope is God using to get me to place all of my hope in Him?

THE ARK ITSELF is submerged, saving the top of it, no foothold anywhere. God removed hope from anywhere but Himself. That is a picture of the kingdom of God when it appears to be completely submerged; yet those very things which look as if they were going to smash it are the things God uses to preserve it.[OPG]

In Doubt: Hope *in* GOD

OUR IDEAS OF God are no greater than ourselves, and we ought to receive from God other ideas by revelation, so that the working mind of man may receive the power to live a larger, grander life than lies in any of his own ideas. Our ideas of God are indistinct, and when we make those ideas in their indistinctness the ground of our understanding of God, we are hopelessly at sea. We are never told to walk in the light of our convictions or instinctive ideas; according to the Bible, we have to walk in the light of Our Lord. As that marvelous Being has His dominant sway over us, the whole of Time, the whole of Eternity, and the threshold between the two, will be shot through with the dawn of an endless day that shall never end in night.[BE]

Reflection Questions

How does the false light of my own convictions keep me from walking in the true light of God's revelation?

IT IS NOT a flimsy, false dream that springs in the human heart, but a real visible paradise of God; that our hope will be abundantly satisfied.[CD]

GOD HAS TO deal with us on the death side as well as on the life side. It is all very well to know in theory that there are things we must not trust in, but another thing to know it in fact. When God deals with us on the death side He puts the sentence of death on everything we should not trust in, and we have a miserable time until we learn never any more to trust in it, never any more to look anywhere else than to God. It sometimes happens that hardly a day passes without God saying, "Don't trust there, that is dead."[GW]

Reflection Questions

What am I most tempted to trust rather than God? Am I more likely to trust myself? others? or God?

THE BEST OF men are but the best of men. Don't glory in men; don't say, I am of Paul; I am of Apollos. Bank your confidence in God, not in men.[SHH]

GOD VISITS THE believer with the word of promise and visits him again with the word of fulfillment. Abraham endured for twenty-five years without any sign of fulfillment. The majority of us know nothing about waiting, we don't wait, we endure. Waiting means that we go on in the perfect certainty of God's goodness. The attitude of the human heart towards God Who promises should be to give Him credit for being honest.NKW

Reflection Questions

What is the difference between waiting and enduring, between wishing and hoping? Which am I more likely to do? What keeps me from standing firm in faith?

GOD IS LOVE, and He will see after us if we stand steadfast to our confidence in Him. It is easy to stand fast in the big things, but very difficult in the small things. If we do stand fast in faith in Him we shall become irresistible disciples.AUG

47

WE MUST BE careful never to compromise over any promise of God when by reason of human limitation there has been only a partial fulfillment. Every word God has spoken will be absolutely fulfilled; to climb down from that confidence is to be disloyal to God. Beware, though, of inferring because no good word of God will fail, that I personally will necessarily partake in its fulfillment.[OPG]

Reflection Questions

What promise of God am I beginning to doubt? Am I certain that it was made to me or was it to someone else? What am I trying to "buy" from God with my virtue?

OUR NATURAL VIRTUES are remnants of what God created man to be, not promises of what he is going to be. The natural virtues cannot be patched up to come anywhere near God's demands, and the sign that God is at work in us is that He corrupts our confidence in the natural virtues. It is simply an amplification of the old Gospel hymn—"Nothing in my hand I bring; Simply to thy cross I cling!"[ITWBP]

In Doubt: Hope *in* GOD

HAVE YOU BEEN saying, "I cannot expect God to do that for me"? Why can't you? Is God Almighty impoverished by your circumstances? Is His hand shortened that it cannot save? Are your particular circumstances so peculiar, so remote from the circumstances of every son and daughter of Adam, that the Atonement and the grace of God are not sufficient for you? When we have the simple, childlike trust in God that Jesus exhibited, the overflowing grace of God will have no limits, and we must set no limits to it.[HG]

Reflection Questions

What doubts, fears, tensions, or unresolved conflicts do I allow in my life even though they keep God from realizing His hope for me?

IT IS A tremendous thing to know that God reigns and rules and rejoices, and that His joy is our strength. The confidence of a Christian is that God never pouts.[PH]

IF WE ARE going to have a sympathetic understanding of the Bible, we must rid ourselves of the abominable conceit that we are the wisest people that have ever been on the earth; we must stop our patronage of Jesus Christ and of the Bible, and have a bigger respect for the fundamental conception of life as it is. At the basis of Hebrew wisdom first of all, is confidence in God.[SHH]

Reflection Questions

In what ways do success and self-confidence stunt the growth of my hope? What possessions keep me from trusting God?

IF YOU HAVE many possessions, it will ruin your trust and make you suspect everyone, and the better type of life is ruined. You cannot find lasting joy in these things, let them come and go, remain true to your relationship to God and don't put your trust in possessions. Trust in God whatever happens, and the result will be that in your heart will be the joy that every man is seeking.[SHH]

In Doubt: Hope *in* GOD

IT IS A snare to continually think about defects. Imagine anyone who has seen himself in the light of Jesus Christ thinking of his defects! Why we are too filthy for words, and to be concerned because of the spots upon us is absurd. Leave the whole miserable thing alone; we have the sentence of death in ourselves that we should not trust in ourselves but in God, and there are no specks in God.[NKW]

Reflection Questions

In what ways do my faults and failures stunt the growth of my hope? What reason do I have for hope if I refuse to grant or accept forgiveness?

THE BACKGROUND OF God's forgiveness is holiness. If God were not holy there would be nothing in His forgiveness. There is no such thing as God overlooking sin; therefore if God forgives there must be a reason that justifies His doing so. In forgiving a man, God gives him the heredity of His own Son—He turns him into the standard of the Forgiver. Forgiveness is a revelation—hope for the hopeless; that is the message of the Gospel.[SA]

JOB HAD PERFECT confidence in the character of God though he did not understand the way He was taking. We sometimes wrongly illustrate faith in God by the faith of a business man. Faith commercially is based on calculation, but religious faith cannot be illustrated by the kind of faith we exhibit in life. Faith in God is a terrific venture in the dark; I have to believe that God is good in spite of all that contradicts it in my experience. It is not easy to say that God is love when everything that happens actually gives the lie to it. Everyone's soul represents some kind of battlefield.[BFB]

Reflection Questions

How do advancements in science and modern civilization minimize my need for hope in God? How does this endanger my spiritual well-being?

JUST AS NATIONS place their confidence for security in armaments or arbitration and neglect the worship of God as the only security, so individuals may easily place confidence in the amenities of society, in civilized entrenchments, in a good home and a good situation, and belittle the one abiding security—in God![CD]

JOB'S STRONG UTTERANCES are not against God, but against the statements of his former creed. The man who will stand true to God behind the expression of his creed is true to his belief *in God*, instead of to the presentation of Him which is in dispute. If you listen to a man who has been sorely hit, he may utter what, to you who have not been hit, sounds blasphemous. Job's claim is that his friends ought to have known that it was not imagination that made him speak as he did, but the fact that he had been desperately hard hit. The only way out for Job is not on the line of reason, but on the line of implicit confidence.[BFB]

Reflection Questions

How do wrong beliefs about God distort my confidence in God? Where have I seen God's grace at work? How has this increased my hope?

JESUS CHRIST NEVER trusted human nature, yet He was never cynical, never in despair about any man, because He trusted absolutely in what the grace of God could do in human nature.[PH]

53

MINISTRY IS THE "glorious gospel of the blessed God, which was committed to my trust." If I am going to be loyal to that trust, I must never allow any impertinent sensitiveness to hinder my keeping the trust. My trust is the glorious gospel for myself and through me to others, and it is realized in two ways: in the perfect certainty that God has redeemed the world, and in the imperative necessity of working on that basis with everyone with whom I come in contact (cf. Col. 1:28–29).[AUG]

Reflection Questions

How is the hope of the gospel being realized in and through me? Do I place more hope in the physical or spiritual realm?

MATHEMATICS IS THE rule of reason and common sense, but faith and hope is the rule of the spiritual. We are gloriously uncertain of the next step, but we are certain of God. Immediately we abandon to God and do the duty that lies nearest, He packs our lives with surprises all the time; whereas if we become the advocates of a set creed something dies.[LG]

In Doubt: Hope *in* GOD

PLANS ARISE FROM the human "must"—the imperative demand of my own undisciplined nature which
makes me feel, "I must do something; God is no use
here." God rarely rebukes us for our impulsive plans because those plans work their own distress. Plans made
apart from trusting God's wisdom are rotten.[OPG]

Reflection Questions

*What lessons have I learned from mistaken
trust? Do my prayers sound more as if I'm
having a contest with God or expressing my
confidence in Him?*

GOD NEVER HEARS prayer because a man is earnest;
He hears and answers prayer that is on the right plat-
form. It is not our agony and our distress, but our childlike confidence in God.[GW]

OUR LORD NEVER trusted any man, but He had the profoundest confidence in what He could do for every man, consequently He was never in a moral or intellectual panic, as we are, because we put our confidence in man and in the things that Jesus put no confidence in. Paul says, "Don't think of yourself more highly than you ought to think, but think according to the measure of faith, that is, according to what the grace of God has done in you." This means that you will never be unkind to anyone, whether it be a degraded criminal or an upright moral man, because you have learned that the only thing to depend on in a man is what God has done in him.[HG]

Reflection Questions
What do my attitude and actions toward the lost reveal about my level of confidence in God's power to save?

WHEN YOU COME to work for Jesus Christ, ask yourself, "Am I as confident in His power as He is in His own?" If without faith in Jesus Christ you try to deal with people it will crush the very life out of you. If we believe in Jesus Christ, we can face every problem the world holds.[HG]

GOD'S HEART IS absolutely at rest now that He has created man; even in spite of the fact of the fall, and all else, God is absolutely confident that everything will turn out as He said it would. The devil has laughed at God's hope for thousands of years, and has ridiculed and scorned that hope, but God is not upset or alarmed about the final issue; He is certain that man will bruise the serpent's head.[BP]

Reflection Questions

Why am I skeptical of those who express confidence that God can redeem, restore, and renew all things and all people?

NO ONE CAN tell you where the shadow of the Almighty is, you must find that out for yourself. When you have found out where it is, stay there; under that shadow no evil can ever befall you. The intensity of the moments spent under the shadow of the Almighty is the measure of your usefulness as a worker. Intensity of communion is not in feelings or emotions or in special places, but in quiet, fixed, confident centering on God.[AUG]

POPULAR CHRISTIANITY SAYS, "We must succeed." The New Testament conception of spirituality in the world is a forlorn hope always, by God's design. In the parable of the Sower, only one-fourth of the seed sown brings forth fruit. We are determined to be successful. whereas the apostle Paul says we are called upon to be faithful (1 Corinthians 4:1–2). We have to remain steadfastly patient to God through the whole thing.^SHL

Reflection Questions

How much of my hope depends on being successful rather than being faithful? Do I base my confidence on God or on my experience with God?

SPIRITUALLY, WHEN AN individual builds his confidence on anything less than God inevitably there will be a perishing of the ground of confidence. Experience is the door to a life. The wonderful thing about real living experience is that it is never referred to as past, but merely as the entrance into what is now enjoyed. Beware of building your faith on your experience of God's grace instead of on God Who makes the experience possible.^NJ

In Doubt: Hope *in* GOD

THE DEVIL LIKES to make us believe that we are in a losing battle. Nothing of the sort! we have to overcome all the things that try to obscure God. The rugged truths of Isaiah point out not only the appalling state of the world as it is, but that we have to live a holy life in it by the power of God, not a sequestered life in particular temples or rituals, but real genuine magnificent men and women of God, no matter what the devil or the world or the flesh may do.[NI]

Reflection Questions

What tools does Satan use to make me feel hopeless? How do feelings of hopelessness affect my worship? What am I missing when I agree to remain hopeless?

THE ONLY THING God is interested in is *life*, He is not interested in religious forms, and this is what the people had forgotten, they only recognized God in their moribund religious services. God is going to make us worthy of the best saints we have known if we go on with Him (Isaiah 29:22–24). All through Isaiah there is the confidence that God is reigning and ruling.[NI]

THE DISTRESS AND agony the prophets experienced was the agony of believing God when everything that was happening contradicted what they proclaimed Him to be; there was nothing to prove that God was just and true, but everything to prove the opposite. The forlorn-hope aspect is the best, perhaps the only idea, for the godly. To walk with God means walking apart from ultimate godless reliances.[OPG]

Reflection Questions

What false hope do I need to give up so that I can have complete confidence in God? What habit competes with hope?

THE CONDITION OF the people is hopeless, habit has become second nature; the day for reformation has gone by. Never trust innocence of outlook in yourself or in other people when the statements of God's word are directly opposite (see Mark 7:21 and Jer. 17:19). We continually trust in ourselves and other people until we have learned to have absolute confidence in God.[NJ]

In Doubt: Hope *in* GOD

THE EXPECTATION OF the heart must be based on this certainty: "in all the world there is none but Thee, my God, there is none but Thee." Until the human heart rests there, every other relationship in life is precarious and will end in heartbreak. There is only one Being Who can satisfy the last aching abyss of the human heart, and that is the Lord Jesus Christ.^{MFL}

Reflection Questions

What does my lack of kindness reveal about my desire for satisfaction from someone other than God? How would my attitude toward people change if all my hope were in God?

THE WHOLE HISTORY of envy and cruelty in human relationships is summed up in the demand for infinite satisfaction from human hearts. We will never get it, and we are apt to become cruel, vindictive, bitter, and often criminal. When once the heart is right with God and the real center of the life satisfied, we never expect or demand infinite satisfaction from a finite heart; we become absolutely kind to all other hearts and never become a snare.^{MFL}

THE EXPLANATION OF Job's suffering is the fact that God and Satan had made a battleground of his soul. It was not for Job's chastening or his perfecting, but for an ulterior purpose that Job did not know. Job's intuition made him stick to the fact that the only One who could explain the sublimities of Nature was the One who could explain what he was going through. Job trusted that God was honorable and just and true, and that he would be justified in sticking to his faith in God's honor, though meantime it looked as if God was deliberately destroying him.[BFB]

Reflection Questions

What battle is going on in my soul? What causes me to lose hope in God's ability to redeem the situation?

THE REASON WE know so little about God's wisdom is that we will only trust Him as far as we can work things out according to our own reasonable commonsense.[OPG]

In Doubt: Hope *in* GOD

THE FORWARD LOOK sees everything in God's perspective whereby His wonderful distance is put on the things that are near. Caleb had the perspective of God; the men who went up with him saw only the inhabitants of the land as giants and themselves as grasshoppers. Learn to take the long view and you will breathe the benediction of God among the squalid things that surround you. Some people never get ordinary or commonplace, they transfigure everything they touch because they have got the forward look which brings their confidence in God into the actual details of life.[CHI]

Reflection Questions

What "giants" are casting a shadow that looks bigger to me than God? How would I live differently if I saw them as mere shadows of something small?

THERE ARE SOME things over which we may lose faith if we have confidence in God's power only. There is so much that looks like the mighty power of God that is not. We must have confidence in God over and above everything He may do.[IYSA]

THE JOY THAT a believer can give to God is the purest pleasure God ever allows a saint, and it is very humiliating to realize how little joy we do give Him. We put our trust in God up to a certain point, then we say, "Now I must do my best." There are times when there is no human best to be done, when the Divine best must be left to work, and God expects those of us who know Him to be confident in His ability and power.[PH]

Reflection Questions

How often am I more concerned about doing something good for God than allowing Him to do something good through me? How does this indicate that I have more hope in myself than in Him?

THE SECURITY OF the eternal God is what we are to have confidence in, and the Psalmist likens that security to the mountains, because a mountain is the most stable thing we know. There is nothing so secure as the salvation of God; it is as eternal as the mountains, and it is our trust in God that brings us the conscious realization of this.[HG]

In Doubt: Hope *in* GOD

THE ONE THING Satan tries to shake is our confidence in God. It is not difficult for our confidence to be shaken if we build on our experience; but if we realize that all we experience is but the doorway leading to the knowledge of God, Satan may shake that as much as he likes, but he cannot shake the fact that God remains faithful (see 2 Tim. 2:13), and we must not cast away our confidence in Him. It is not our trust that keeps us, but the God in whom we trust who keeps us. We are always in danger of trusting in our trust, believing our belief, having faith in our faith. All these things can be shaken; we have to base our faith on those things which cannot be shaken (see Heb. 12:27).[HG]

Reflection Questions

How can I distinguish between my confidence in God's blessings and my confidence in God himself?

THE KNOWLEDGE OF the real God is reached when my confidence is placed in God and not in His blessings.[NKW]

THE ONLY PLACE of confidence is personal trust in God and patient waiting for Him. One of the things we have to unlearn is the idea of judgment which never came from God's Book, that is, the idea that God is vindictive. Our Lord never spoke from personal vindictiveness, He spoke from a knowledge of the eternal principles of God, which are inexorable. To trust in the goodness of God is not enough, it is not eternal and abiding; we have to trust *God,* who is infinitely more than goodness.[NI]

Reflection Questions

If I truly believe that God is better than the best, and more powerful than the greatest, why do I still trust my own understanding of things?

THERE ARE EXPERIENCES in human lives which are not part of God's purpose, but the result of human perversity. Remember, trust in God does not mean that God will explain His solutions to us, it means that we are perfectly confident in God, and when we do see the solution we find it to be in accordance with all that Jesus Christ revealed of His character.[OPG]

THE STRENGTH OF life is not in the certainty that we can do the thing, but in the perfect certainty that God will. We are certain only of the One Whom we are trusting. The strength of our life lies in knowing that our strength is in God. "And to know the love of Christ"—its breadth, and length, and depth, and height, we cannot get out of it anywhere. When we know the love of Christ, which passes knowledge, it means that we are free from anxiety, free from carefulness, so that during the twenty-four hours of the day we do what we ought to do all the time, with the strength of life bubbling up with real spontaneous joy.[LG]

Reflection Questions

What faulty ideas do I have about strength that affect my joy? What faulty beliefs about love affect my confidence in God?

THERE IS NO more glorious opportunity than the day in which we live for proving in personal life and in every way that we are confident in God.[PH]

NOTHING IN LIFE is certain. We may say that if a man has been well brought up and has developed his own integrity and lived rightly, success will be sure to attend him, but you cannot calculate along that line. Certain things cannot be explained. There is a wildness in things and if God does not step in and adjust it, there is no hope; but God has stepped in by the Redemption, and our part is to trust confidently in Him.[BFB]

Reflection Questions

Scientists can observe the way things are, but only God knows the way they're supposed to be. Why then would I let my hope in God take second place to science?

THERE IS A wildness all through Nature and we are suddenly struck with its brutality and ask, "Why, if God is a beneficent Creator, does He allow such diabolical things to happen?" The Bible explanation is that Nature is in a disorganized condition, that it is out of gear with God's purposes, and will only become organized when God and man are one (see Rom. 8:19). The great thing is to remain absolutely confident in God.[GW]

In Doubt: Hope *in* GOD

SOME TRY BY aspiration and prayer and consecration and obedience, built up from looking at the lives that stand like mountain peaks, to attain a similarity of character, and they are woefully lagging behind; they falter by the way, and the characters that used to stir intense hopefulness leave the soul sighing. To such a reader let the message be: A strong saintly character is not the production of human breeding or culture, it is the manufacture of God.[PH]

Reflection Questions

What does lack of hope in God cause me to try doing on my own? How does lack of confidence in God's timing make me impatient?

THERE WILL COME one day a personal and direct touch from God when every tear and perplexity, every oppression and distress, every suffering and pain, and wrong and justice will have a complete and ample and overwhelming explanation. The Christian faith is exhibited by the man who has the spiritual courage to say that that is the God he trusts in, and it takes some moral backbone to do it. It is easier to attempt to judge everything in the span between birth and death.[SHH]

IT IS NOT easy to have faith in God, and it is not meant to be easy because we have to make character. God will shield us from no requirements of His sons and daughters any more than He shielded His own Son. It is an easy business to sit in an armchair and say, "Oh yes, I believe God will do this and that"; that is credulity, not faith. But let me say, "I believe God will supply all my needs," and then let me "run dry," no money, no outlook, and see whether I will go through the trial of my faith, or sink back and put my trust in something else. If we go through the trial, there is so much wealth laid up in our heavenly banking account to draw upon when the next test comes.[HG]

Reflection Questions

How will my hope have any substance if it's not put to the test? How can I claim to believe God if I've never had reason to doubt?

THINK OF THE thousands who have had to go through tribulation during these past years—every human hope taken from them; but yet the saint with an amazing hope-fulness remains radiant in the thick of it.[CD]

IT IS VERY easy to trust in God when there is no difficulty, but that is not trust at all, it is simply letting the mind rest in a complacent mood; but when there is sickness in the house, when there is trouble, when there is death, where is our trust in God? The clearest evidence that God's grace is at work in our hearts is that we do not get into panics.[CD]

Reflection Questions

What do my emotional reactions tell me about my confidence in God? What do they tell God about me? Why do I insist on being heard when it's more important for me to be still so I can hear?

WOULD WE REALLY hear God's Word, or are we not rather in this immediate tribulation waiting for God to persuade us that our own way is right after all? Oh, the bliss of that disciplined child-heart, which when He speaks, says, "Yes, Lord," and simply obeys.[CD]

EVERY TIME YOU venture out on the life of faith, you will come across something that seems to contradict what your faith in God says you should believe. Go through the trial of faith and lay up your confidence in God, not in your common sense, and you will gain wealth in your heavenly banking account, and the more you go through the trial of faith the wealthier you will become in the heavenly regions. You will go through difficulties smilingly, and men will wonder where your wealth of trust comes from.^SSM

Reflection Questions
What kind of wealth makes me feel secure?
What does this reveal about the basis
of my hope?

THE TRIAL OF our faith gives us a good banking account in the heavenly places, and when the next trial comes our wealth there will tide us over. If we have confidence in God beyond the actual earthly horizons, we shall see the lie at the heart of the fear and our faith will win through in every detail.^HSGM

ABRAHAM'S ABERRATIONS SPRANG not from disobedience, but from trusting in his own wits. Directly God's command was made known to him, he obeyed; when there was no command he was inclined to trust in his wits, and that is where he went wrong. It is never right to do wrong in order that right may come, although it may seem justifiable from every standard saving one. In the long run you can never produce right by doing wrong, yet we will always try to do it unless we believe what the Bible says. If I tell a lie in order to bring about the right, I prove to my own conviction that I do not believe the One at the back of the universe is truthful.^{OPG}

Reflection Questions

What lies do I tell because I would rather trust the imaginary protection of falsehood than the real but vulnerable protection of truth?

JUDGE EVERYTHING IN the light of Jesus Christ, who is the Truth, and you will never do the wrong thing however right it looks.^{OPG}

WHENEVER WE START doubtful weighing of things we are acting not in accordance with our reliance on God, but in presumptuous confidence that God will see us through if we trust our wits: God will see us through only if we stand steadfastly true to what He has told us. Another danger is to imagine that it is my particular presentation of things that will attract people. It may attract them, but never to God. The line of attraction is always an indication of the goal of the attracted; if you attract by personal impressiveness, the attracted will get no further than you.[NKW]

Reflection Questions

In what realms do I try to attract people to myself rather than to God? How might this cause them to rely more on me than on God?

WHAT IS NEEDED today is not a new gospel, but men and women who can re-state the Gospel of the Son of God in terms that will reach the very heart of our problems. Today men are flinging the truth overboard as well as the terms. Our hope for usefulness is in men and women saturated with the truth of God who can re-state the old truth in terms that appeal to our day.[AUG]

OUR FUSS OVER other souls is nearly always evidence that we have not the slightest trust in God. Our Lord never made a fuss over anyone, and the reason He didn't could not have been that He was callous or indifferent, or that He was not tenderhearted, or that He did not understand every detail, but the fact remains that He did not make a fuss over anyone. He never pleaded, He never cajoled, He never entrapped; He simply spoke the sternest words mortal ears ever heard, and then let it alone.[GW]

Reflection Questions
What begging and pleading do I need to stop?
What simple acts of faith should I do instead?

NEVER SHRINK FROM dealing with any life you are brought up against, but never go unless you are quite sure God wants you to, He will guide. God's permission means there is no shadow of doubt on the horizon of consciousness; when there is, wait. God never guides by fogs or by lightning flashes, He guides naturally.[DI]

ONE OF THE greatest strains in life is the strain of waiting for God. God takes the saints like a bow which He stretches and at a certain point the saint says, "I can't stand any more," but God does not heed, He goes on stretching because He is aiming at His mark, not ours, and the patience of the saints is that they "hang in" until God lets the arrow fly.[GW]

Reflection Questions

In what ways am I being stretched? How would it be less stressful if I would relax and not resist? Why do I feel as if I must run when I am in trouble rather than stand steadfastly?

STAND STEADFASTLY TRUE to God, and God will bring His truth out in a way that will make your life a sacrament, i.e., the abiding presence of God will come through the simple elements of your life, but you must wait for Him.[GW]

WE CANNOT ATTAIN a vision, we must live in the inspiration of it until it accomplishes itself. We get so practical that we forget the vision. At the beginning we saw the vision but did not wait for it; we rushed off into practical work, and when the vision was fulfilled, we did not see it. Waiting for the vision that tarries is the test of our loyalty to God. It is at the peril of our soul's welfare that we get caught up in practical work and miss the fulfillment of the vision.^{CG}

Reflection Questions

What am I unwilling to wait for? What do I risk losing if I try to acquire it in my own way and in my own strength? What is one thing I know God wants me to do? When will I start doing it?

WAIT ON GOD and He will work, but don't wait in spiritual sulks because you cannot see an inch in front of you! Are we detached enough from our own spiritual hysterics to wait on God? To wait is not to sit with folded hands, but to learn to do what we are told.^{CG}

As YOU WAIT only upon God, concentrating on the glorious outlines of His salvation, there will come into you the sleeping peace of God, the certainty that you are in the place where God is doing all in accordance with His will. In this earnest life of communion with God, the stress of the life is in the right place, that is, you are not in earnest in order that God may recognize you as His child; your earnestness is the outcome of real communion with God.PH

Reflection Questions

*Why do I hurry? What is so important that
I can't find time to spend with God and
concentrate on all the work He has done
without my help?*

STOP ALL FALSE hurry and spend time in communion with God. Think of the benediction which comes to your disposition by waiting upon God! Some of us are in such a hurry that we distort God's blessings for ourselves and for others.PH

FANATICISM IS STICKING true to my interpretation of my destiny instead of waiting for God to make it clear. The fanatical line is—*Do* something; the test of faith lies in *not* doing. Fanaticism is always based on the highest I believe; a sordid being is never fanatical. Our Lord taught His disciples to pray—"Lead us not into temptation." To say—"Lord, I will do whatever You tell me to do; I will stand loyal to You," is deliberately to disobey this caution of Our Lord.[NKW]

Reflection Questions

What am I afraid of not doing? What am I unwilling to stop doing? What justification or vindication am I striving for? What am I trying to prove about myself because God seems slow in doing it?

THE EARNEST EXPECTATION of the creation waits for the revealing of the sons of God (Romans 8:19). For that great hour we hope and long, when we shall pass from beneath the Shade of His Hand into the full Shine of His Face.[SHH]

IT IS A crucial point in practical spiritual experience when we learn not to be more eager to do God's will than He is for us to do it. Our zeal to serve God may be and often is our insistence on God proving that our way is right; we see what God's will is as we wait before Him, and then we hurry up circumstances in order to do it, and we receive a severe punishment at the hand of God. God will put us in circumstances where we have to take steps of which we do not see the meaning, only on looking back do we discern that it was God's will for us.[NE]

Reflection Questions

How much energy do I put into trying to get God's approval for my plans? Am I willing to be obedient if it means doing nothing but wait?

GOD GRANT THAT in times of perplexity we may get back again to the watch-tower, back again to inspired waiting, back again to the wide-eyed wonder of a child at God's answers to our prayers.[IYSA]

In Doubt: Hope *in* GOD

MOST OF US are at our wits' end. We have no inkling of what God is doing because our eyes have not been waiting upon Him. We are apt to pay more attention to our newspaper than to God's Book, and spiritual leakage begins because we do not make the effort to lift up our eyes to God. "But we all, with open face beholding as in a glass the glory of the Lord, are changed into the same image from glory to glory" (2 Cor. 3:13). That is a description of entire reliance on God.[HG]

Reflection Questions

How much of my confusion and frustration has to do with my failure to wait and find out what God is doing?

THE MEANING OF waiting in both the Old and New Testament is "standing under," actively enduring. It is not standing with folded arms doing nothing; it is not saying, "In God's good time it will come to pass"—that often means in my abominably lazy time I let God work. Waiting means standing under, in active strength, enduring till the answer comes.[IYSA]

THE MEASURE OF the worth of our public activity to God is the private, profound communion we have with Him. Rush is always wrong; there is plenty of time to worship God. There are not three stages—worship, waiting, and work; some of us go in jumps like spiritual frogs, we jump from worship to waiting and from waiting to work. God's idea is that the three should go together; they were always together in the life of Our Lord, He was unhasting and unresting. It is a discipline, we cannot get there all at once.[NKW]

Reflection Questions

What needless and futile rushing do I build into my life because it makes me feel important? What part do worship, work, and rest play in my life? Do they compete for attention or work together as a team?

THE TEMPTATION IS to work up enthusiasm, to kindle a fire of our own and walk in the light of it. We have to stay on God and wait. Never try to help God to fulfill His word.[SSIY]

WE ARE APT to look upon uncertainty as a bad thing, because we are all too mathematical. We imagine we have to reach an end; but a particular end is not of the nature of spiritual life. The nature of spiritual life is that we are certain in our uncertainty, consequently we do not make our "nests" anywhere spiritually. Immediately we make a "nest" out of an organization or a creed or a belief, we come across the biggest of all calamities.[LG]

Reflection Questions
In what ways do I treat God like a mathematical formula? What is wrong with hope that is based on belief in a God who is restricted by natural law?

WHENEVER I BECOME certain of my creeds, I kill the life of God in my soul, because I cease to believe in God and believe in my belief instead. All through the Bible the realm of the uncertain is the realm of joy and delight; the certainty of belief brings distress.[LG]

WE HAVE TO build in absolute confidence on God. There is nothing more heroic than to have faith in God when you can see so many better things in which to have faith. It is comparatively easy to have faith in God in a pathetic way in the starvation of things round about you, but a different matter to have faith in God after a tremendous victory has been won, and then in the aftermath that follows to think that there is to be no realization of that for which God had caused you to hope.NKW

Reflection Questions

How does spiritual victory undermine my hope in God? In what ways do I take credit for the work God has done?

WHAT A WONDERFUL picture—a group of our Lord's children around the knees of the Heavenly Father, making their requests known in familiarity, in awe and reverence, in simplicity and confidence in Him, and in humble certainty that He is there.CD

WHAT COUNTS IN a man's life is the disposition that rules him. When God begins His work in us He does not make a mighty difference in our external lives, but He shifts the center of our confidence; instead of relying on ourselves and other people, we rely on God, and are kept in perfect peace. We all know the difference it makes if we have someone who believes in us and in whom we believe, there is no possibility of being crushed.[AUG]

Reflection Questions

Am I more concerned about God's work in my circumstances or in my soul? Where is God devoting most of His time? What does this tell me about where I should focus my attention?

WHEN A MAN or woman's heart is strong in confidence in God, there is no snare in earthly friendship because the heart is at rest with God, and there are no areas of desert and wilderness.[NJ]

WHEN YOU ARE learning to trust God, He gives you at first certain things you lean on; then He withdraws, and you say it is the devil. No, it is the chastening of the Lord because He sees that you are possessing those things. You can only possess your possessions by being detached from them to God Who is the Source. If you are drawing your life from God and begin to take a wrong line, God will withdraw His life. This is also true with regard to money. We have only one Source, and that is God. One of the biggest snares is the idea that God is sure to lead us to success.^{NKW}

Reflection Questions

How does success figure into my concept of hope? How does my idea of success conflict with God's?

WHEN JESUS SAYS, "Come unto Me," I simply come; when He says "Trust God in this matter," I do not try to trust, I *do* trust.^{NKW}

YOU DO NOT choose your own heredity or your own disposition, these things are beyond your control, and yet these are the things which influence you. You may rake the bottom of the universe, but you cannot explain things; they are wild, there is nothing rational about them. We cannot get to the bottom of things; we cannot get behind the before of birth or the after of death; therefore the wise man is the one who trusts the wisdom of God, not his own wits.[SHH]

Reflection Questions

What happens to my confidence in God when I allow myself to believe that I should be able to understand everything He does or doesn't do? What happens when I convince myself that God will reveal to me everything I need to know at the time I need to know it?

WHILE WE ARE "climbing the slow ascensions" of our Heavenly Father's wisdom, He engineers our circumstances by His providence and puts within our inmost soul the childlike joy of confidence in himself.[OPG]

REMEMBER, YOU ARE not the designer of your destiny. You hear the call of God and realize what He wants, then you begin to find reasons why you should not obey. Well, obey Him, because away in some other part of the world there are other circumstances being worked by God, and if you say, "I wasn't made for this," you get out of touch with God. Your "goings" are not according to your mind, but according to God's mind. Remain true to what God is doing. The Almighty has got you in hand, leave yourself alone and trust in Him.^{NKW}

Reflection Questions

Why is it foolish for me to try to convince God to change how He is handling a situation? What might be the ripple effects if God were to order the universe according to my whims?

"THE HOPE OF His calling" is the great light on every problem. God grant that we "will come unto Him, and make Our abode with Him," the triune God abiding with the saint. What does a man need to care after that!^{IYSA}

THE CALL OF God only becomes clear as we obey, never as we weigh the *pros* and *cons* and try to reason it out. When we hear the call of God it is not for us to dispute with God, and arrange to obey Him if He will expound the meaning of His call to us. As long as we insist on having the call expounded to us, we will never obey; but when we obey it is expounded, and in looking back there comes a chuckle of confidence. Before us there is nothing, but overhead there is God, and we have to trust Him.^{NKW}

Reflection Questions

What question am I waiting for God to answer?
What command is God waiting for me to obey?

WHEN ONCE A saint puts confidence in the election of God, no tribulation or affliction can ever touch that confidence. When we realize that there is no hope of deliverance in human wisdom, or in human rectitude, or in anything that we can do, then we accept the justification of God and to stand true to the election of God in Christ Jesus. This is the finest cure for spiritual degeneration.^{CD}

DON'T BE DISTURBED today by thoughts about to-morrow. Leave tomorrow alone, and bank in confidence on God's organization of what you do not see. God re-makes things beautiful when He gets His time in us over again. In our "teens" we begin to get into the throes of life and we lose our sense of the beauty of things, and only when we get into a personal relationship with God do we find again that everything is beautiful.[SHH]

Reflection Questions

What do I have today that I don't appreciate because of my fear of tomorrow? What keeps me from seeing the beauty of life? How do things "seen" keep me from appreciating the "unseen"?

IT IS NOT faith when you trust in what you see; faith is trusting in what you don't see, hanging in to the God whose character you know though meantime there is no evidence that He is at work on your behalf.[NI]

HAVING FAITH TESTS a man for all he is worth. He has to stand in the midst of things which conflict with his faith, and place his confidence in the God Whose character is revealed in Jesus Christ. Jesus Christ's statements reveal that God is a Being of love and justice and truth; our immediate circumstances seem to prove He is not; are we going to remain true to the revelation that God is good? If we are, we shall find that God in His providence makes the two universes, the universe of revelation and the universe of common sense, work together in perfect harmony.ˢˢᴹ

Reflection Questions

When what I experience conflicts with what God says is true, what do I believe? What do I know about God that gives me reason for hope?

FATE IS SUPERSTITIOUS yielding to a person whose character we do not know and have not the slightest confidence in but have succumbed to. Faith is the process by which our confidence is built up in a Person Whose character we know, however perplexing the present things may be that He is doing.ᴺᴶ

IF WE ARE going to obey God we have to deliberately trust the character of God as it has been revealed to us in the face of all obstacles. "If God would only come down and explain everything to me, I would have faith in Him," we say; and yet how little trust we are inclined to have in God, even when we have had an experience of His grace and a revelation of himself. We sink back to the experience instead of being confident in the God Who gave us the experience. Experience is never the ground of our trust, it is the gateway to the One Whom we trust.[NKW]

Reflection Questions

Do I hope for some kind of experience with God to dispel my doubt or do I experience the hope of God through times of doubt?

MUCH THAT WE call the trial of our faith is the inevitable result of being alive. The problem lies in the clearing of God's character with regard to what He allows. Faith according to the Bible is confidence in God when He is inscrutable and apparently contradictory in His providences.[NKW]

OUR LORD NEVER teaches first by principles, but by personal relationship to himself. When through His Redemption we become rightly related to Him personally, our hearts are unshakably confident in Him. That is the Divine anticipation being participated in, the tremendous work of God's supernatural grace being manifested in our mortal flesh.[CHI]

Reflection Questions

How is God's grace being manifested in me? In what ways does this grace give hope to others? Do the words "complete," "passionate," and "earnest" describe my hope in God?

FAITH IS MORE than an attitude of the mind; faith is the complete, passionate, earnest trust of our whole nature in the Gospel of God's grace as presented in the Life and Death and Resurrection of our Lord Jesus Christ.[OBH]

YOU CANNOT TRUST innocence or natural goodness; you cannot trust possibilities. This explains Jesus
Christ's attitude. Our Lord trusted no man (see John
2:24–25), yet He was never suspicious, never bitter;
His confidence in what God's grace could do for any
man was so perfect that He never despaired of anyone.
If our trust is placed in human beings, we will end in
despairing of every one. But when we limit our thinking
to the things of purity we shall think only of what God's
grace has done in others, and put our confidence in
that and in nothing else.^{MFL}

Reflection Questions

*If I feel that certain people are hopeless, what
does that indicate about my hope in God? What
grace do I see at work in others? How does that
grace affect my sense of hope?*

THE GRACE WE had yesterday won't do for today; but
we can always reckon there is plenty more to draw on
(see 2 Cor. 5:18–21).^{AUG}

WHEN LOOKING BACK on the lives of men and women of God the tendency is to say—"What wonderfully astute wisdom they had! How perfectly they understood all God wanted!" The astute mind behind is the Mind of God, not human wisdom at all. We give credit to human wisdom when we should give credit to the Divine guidance of God through childlike people who were foolish enough to trust God's wisdom and the supernatural equipment of God.^{CG}

Reflection Questions

In what ways do I trust the wisdom and insight of others more than I trust God? Who do I go to for guidance before going to God?

PETER DOES NOT say "give an explanation," but "a reason of the hope that is in you." Be ready to say what you base your hope on. Faith is deliberate confidence in the character of God Whose ways you cannot understand at the time.^{AUG}

GOD IS LOVE. No one but God could have revealed *that* to the world, for we see nothing but its contradiction in our own limited world of experience. No wonder the carnal mind, the merely intellectually cultured, consider us infatuated, mere dreamers, talking of love when murder and war and famine and lust and pestilence, and all the refinement of selfish cruelty is abroad in the earth. But, oh the sublimity of faith that dares to place its action and hope in an unseen and apparently unknown God, saying, "God is love," in spite of all appearances to the contrary.[LG]

Reflection Questions
How does the knowledge that God is love (not "God is loving") change my attitude about my circumstances? What can I hope for because God is my Father?

GOD IS MY Father, He loves me, I can never think of anything He will forget, why should I worry? Nothing happens in any particular unless God's mind is behind it, so we can rest in perfect confidence.[SSM]

In Doubt: Hope *in* GOD

ALL GOD ASKS of me is that I trust Him. When I stop telling God what I want, He can catch me up for what He wants without hindrance. He can crumple me up or exalt me, He can do anything He chooses. He simply asks me to have implicit faith in himself and in His goodness. Self-pity is of the devil; if I go off on that line I cannot be used by God for His purpose in the world. I have "a world within the world" in which I live, and God will never be able to get me outside it because I am afraid of being frost-bitten.CG

Reflection Questions

Do I spend more time telling God what I want or asking God what He wants? What is God's hope for me? How might God want to use me to counteract the effects of sin?

CHRISTIANS HAVE HOPE despite living in alien territory. God is working out His tremendous purpose for the overthrow of everything Satan and sin can do. Everything that sin and Satan have ruined is going to be reconstructed and readjusted through the marvelous Redemption of our Lord Jesus Christ.PS

THE WORK OF a servant of God is to lift up the despairing and the hopeless. The surest sign that God is at work is that He brings the weak to us—the very class we don't want—with the pain and the distress and limitation. We want the strong and robust, and God gathers the feeble-minded, the afflicted and weak. Pain in God's service always leads to glory. We want success, God wants glory. Some of us have the notion that we are saved and sanctified to have a holy hilarious time before God and among men. We are saved and sanctified to be the servants of men.[NI]

Reflection Questions

Am I more interested in my own success or God's glory? Am I willing to serve those who seem the most hopeless or only those who seem to have a glimmer of hope?

IF WE RECOGNIZE that God is taking us into His purposes, we shall no longer try to find out what His purposes are. If we have a purpose of our own it destroys the simplicity that ought to characterize the children of God.[CG]

In Doubt: Hope *in* GOD

THE LORD'S PURPOSE for the disciples was that they should see Him walking on the sea. We have an idea that God is leading us to a certain goal; He is not. The question of getting to a particular end is a mere incident. What men call the process, God calls the end. If in the midst of the turmoil you can remain calm because you see Jesus, that is God's purpose in your life; not that you may say, "I have done this and that." God's purpose for you is that you depend on Him and His power *now;* that you see Him walking on the waves — no shore in sight, no success, just the absolute certainty that it is all right because you see Him.[GW]

Reflection Questions

Do I place my hope in reaching a certain goal or in being faithful to the call of God? Do I have more hope in my list of accomplishments or in Christ's accomplishment on my behalf?

THERE ARE GREAT perplexities in life, but, thank God, if we will trust with bold, implicit trust in the Son of God, He will bring out His perfect, complete purposes in and through our lives.[CD]

Hope: *A* Holy Promise

WHEN I COMPLAIN and say, "Why does God allow this?" I am not only useless but dangerous. Telling God what He should do, that men are being lost and that He ought to save them, is a terrific charge against God, it means that He must be asleep. When God gets me to realize that I am being taken up into *His* enterprises, then I get rest of soul. The great campaign is God's, not mine.[PH]

Reflection Questions

How do my feelings of hopelessness hinder God's work in my life and in the world? How is my hope diminished because I do not take seriously the work of prayer?

PRAYER IS LABOR, not agony, but labor on the ground of our Lord's Redemption in simple confidence in Him. Prayer is simple to us because it cost Him so much to make it possible to us. God grant that we may work His victories for Him by taking His way about it.[IYSA]

HAPPINESS IS A thing that comes and goes, it can never be an end in itself; holiness, not happiness, is the end of man. The great design of God in the creation of man is that he might "glorify God and enjoy Him forever." A man never knows joy until he gets rightly related to God. Satan's claim is that he can make a man satisfied without God, but all he succeeds in doing is to give happiness and pleasure, never joy. Our lives mean much more than we can tell, they fulfill some purpose of God about which we know nothing; our part is to trust in the Lord with all our heart and not lean to our own understanding. BSG

Reflection Questions

Do I spend more time and energy pursuing my "right" to happiness or God's call to righteousness? If all I'm hoping for is happiness, what am I in danger of missing?

EARTHLY WISDOM CAN never come near the threshold of the Divine; if we stop short of the Divine we stop short of God's purpose for our lives.BSG

IF WE SAY "I want to know why I should do this," it means we have no faith in God, but only sordid confidence in our own wits. "If God would only give me supernatural touches, I would trust Him." No, we would idolize ourselves. "I do not mind being a saint if I can remain natural and be a saint entirely on my own initiative." All along it is the hesitation of the natural refusing to be transformed into the spiritual.[NKW]

Reflection Questions
What am I waiting for God to do for me before I am willing to allow Him to do something through me? What if God is waiting to do something through me before doing something for me?

THE DISCIPLINE OF guidance by God's sympathy leads to a clearer, better understanding of God's ideas and hopes and aims. In this way He makes known to us His *ways*; otherwise we simply know His *acts*.[CD]

CONFESSION MEANS WE have trusted God for this thing and we believe on the ground of His word that the work is done. We realize by confessing that we have no one saving God to stand by us. When we believe with the heart, we have to confess with our mouth what we believe to those whose business it is to know. The reason some of us lack assurance is because we do not continue in what we have tested.[OBH]

Reflection Questions

In addition to what I confess about myself to God, what do I need to confess to others about God? What have others confessed to me about God that has strengthened my hope in God?

WE GIVE CREDIT to human wisdom when we should give credit to the Divine guidance of God through child-like people who were foolish enough in the eyes of the world to trust God's wisdom and supernatural equipment, while watching carefully their own steadfast relationship to Him.[SSIY]

JESUS CHRIST TEACHES us to build our confidence in the abiding reality of himself in the midst of everything. If a man puts his confidence in the things which must go, imagine his incomprehensible perplexity when they do go. Our true life is not in the things which are passing, and if we build ourselves on God and His word, when they go, the marvel is that we are not scared. The thing to examine spiritually is, am I connected with Jesus Christ personally? If I have only a form of belief or a creed, all that may go when the elemental trouble comes and I shall have nothing to cling to, but if I build my "house" on the words of Jesus and do them, then no matter what happens I shall find I am founded upon the Rock.[HSGM]

Reflection Questions
Is my hope built on the solid rock of truth or the fluid ideas of my own imagination?

"MY WORD . . . SHALL not return unto Me void"— that is the perennial, unbreakable hope of the preacher; he knows the power of the word of God and he builds his confidence nowhere else but in God.[GW]

THE EXQUISITE BEAUTY of mountain scenery awakens lofty aspirations; the limitless spaces above the high mountain peaks, the snow-clad summit, and the scarred side ending in foliage and beauty as it sweeps to the valley below, stand as a symbol for all that is high and lofty and aspiring. But soon we realize the limitation not only of physical life but also the inner life; the remembrance of mountains and mountain-top experiences leaves us a little wistful. This brings to mind the Psalmist's song: "Shall I lift up mine eyes to the hills?" "Is that where my help will come from?" And the Psalmist answers, "No, my help comes from the Lord Who made the hills!"[PH]

Reflection Questions

What personal limitations—physical, spiritual, emotional—make me wistful? What do I hope to do for God that I think requires more strength than He is able to give me?

HERE IS THE essence of spiritual truth. Not to the great things God has done, not to the noble saints and noble lives He has made, but to God himself do we look for our hope.[PH]

GOD APPEALS TO Elihu and Job to come before Him on the basis of their actual knowledge, and while being true to the facts they know, to leave room for facts they do not know. The still small voice is an appeal not to a superstitious belief in God, but to the actuality of God to man. God disposes altogether of a relationship to himself born of superstitious dread. God counsels Job—"Don't come to too hasty a conclusion, but gird up your loins like a man and wait. You have done right so far in that you would not have Me misrepresented, but you must recognize that there are facts you do not know, and wait for Me to give the revelation of them on the ground of your moral obedience."[BFB]

Reflection Questions

What causes my impatience? Why am I afraid to wait on God? How does waiting fit my definition of hope?

THE WORKER HAS to have discernment like that of a farmer, that is, he must know how to watch, how to wait, and how to work with wonder. The farmer does not wait with folded arms but with intense activity, he keeps at it industriously until the harvest.[AUG]

JOB WOULD NOT bow before God on the basis of superstition; he could not conceive such a God to be worthy. The ground of appeal is not that God says I must do a certain thing, but that I recognize that what God says is likely to be right. Jesus Christ never coerced anyone; He never used supernatural powers, or what we understand by revivals; He refused to stagger human wits into submission to himself.[BFB]

Reflection Questions

When all the systems I rely on fail, what will keep me from using deceit or coercion to get what I need? Without hope in God, what desperate thing would I do to survive?

YOU CANNOT BANK on insurance, or speculations, or on any kind of calculation; you can bank on only one thing, that your interim of life may at any second be cut short; therefore your only confidence is to remain true to God.[SHH]

THE MAJORITY OF us know nothing about the Redemption of forgiveness until we are enmeshed by a personal problem—something stabs us wide awake and we get our indifferent hide pierced; we come up against things and our conscience is roused. When our conscience is roused we know that God dare not forgive us, and it awakens a sense of hopelessness. Forgiveness is a revelation—hope for the hopeless; that is the message of the Gospel.[HSGM]

Reflection Questions
What hope do I have because God dared to forgive me? What hope would I have if He had not?

THE FAITH OF the saints is, as it were, a God-given sixth sense which takes hold on the spiritual facts that are revealed in the Bible. The hope of the saint is the expectation and certainty of human nature transfigured by faith. Hope not transfigured by faith dies. Hope without faith loses itself in vague speculation, but the hope of the saints transfigured by faith endures "as seeing Him Who is invisible."[CD]

NATURALLY WE NEVER look to Nature for illustrations of the spiritual life, we look at the methods of business men, at man's handiwork. Our Lord drew all His illustrations from His Father's handiwork, He spoke of lilies and trees and grass and sparrows. As Christians we have to feast our souls on the things ignored by practical people. A false spirituality blots Nature right out. The way to keep your spiritual life un-panicky, free from hysterics and fuss, free from flagging and breaking, is to consider the bits of God's created universe you can see *where you are.*[NI]

---

*R*eflection *Q*uestions

What reasons for hope do I see in creation?
Why is it important that I take the time to look for them?

FOSTER YOUR LIFE on God and on His creation and you will find a new use for Nature. Read the life of Jesus—the calm, unhasting, unperturbed majesty of His life is like the majesty of the stars in their courses because both are upheld by the same power.[NI]

THE HOPE OF the saint gives the true value to the things seen and temporal—in fact the real enjoyment of things seen and temporal is alone possible to the saint because he sees them in their true relationship to God, and the sickening emptiness of the worldly-minded who grasp the things seen and temporal as though they were eternal, is unknown to him. The characteristic of the saint is not so much the renunciation of the things seen and temporal as the perfect certainty that these things are but the shows of reality.[CD]

Reflection Questions

In what ways do I get confused as to the nature of reality? Do I think of physical things or spiritual things as being more real?

THE PATIENCE OF hope does not turn men and women into monks and nuns, it gives men and women the right use of this world from another world's standpoint.[CD]

TO BE CERTAIN of God means that we are delight-
fully uncertain in all our ways, we do not know what a
day may bring forth. That is generally said with a sigh
of sadness, but it should be rather an expression of
breathless unexpectedness. It is exactly the state of
mind we should be in spiritually, a state of expectant
wonder, like a child. When we are certain of God we
always live in this delightful uncertainty; whereas if we
are certain of our beliefs we never expect to see God
anywhere.[LG]

Reflection Questions

*What am I expecting from God? Am I looking
for certainty in this life or am I anticipating
the excitement of discovering where God will
show up next? In what way does my impatience
indicate my misplaced hope?*

PATIENCE IS THE result of well-centered strength. To
"wait on the Lord," and to "rest in the Lord," is an indication of a healthy, holy faith.[CD]

THE STARS DO their work without fuss; God does His work without fuss, and saints do their work without fuss. The people who are always desperately active are a nuisance; it is through the saints who are one with Him that God is doing things all the time. The broken and the jaded and the twisted are being ministered to by God through the saints who are not overcome by their own panic, who because of their oneness with Him are absolutely at rest, consequently He can work through them. A sanctified saint remains perfectly confident in God, because sanctification is not something the Lord gives me, sanctification is *himself in me*.[PH]

Reflection Questions

What does my fear of rest say to God about my confidence in Him? What does my refusal to rest say to the world about the source of my hope?

A SANCTIFIED SAINT is at leisure from himself and his own affairs, confident that God is bringing all things out well.[PH]

In Despair

Hope *in the* Spirit

WHEN YOU COME to a crisis there are two distinct ways before you, one the way of ordinary, strong, moral, common sense and the other the way of waiting on God until the mind is formed which can understand His will. Any amount of backing will be given you for the first line, the backing of worldly people and of semi-Christian people, but you will feel the warning, the drawing back of the Spirit of God.[BP]

Reflection Questions

How can I discern whether a prompting is from God or from my own desire for popularity or power? How can I discern when God is speaking to me through other people?

IF YOU WAIT on God, study His Word, and watch Him at work in your circumstances, you will be brought to a decision along God's line, and your worldly "backers" and your semi-Christian "backers" will fall away from you with disgust and say, "It is absurd, you are getting fanatical."[BP]

In Despair: Hope *in the* SPIRIT

TAKE HEED THAT you do not allow carnal suspicion to take the place of the discernment of the Spirit. Fruit and fruit alone is the test. Jesus says you will not gather thistles from any root but a thistle root; but remember that it is quite possible in winter time to mistake a rose tree for something else, unless you are expert in judging. So there is a place for patience, and our Lord would have us heed this. Wait for the fruit to manifest itself and do not be guided by your own fancy.^{SSM}

Reflection Questions

What do I hope to accomplish by rushing to judgment? Why do I think that being quick to judge is better than judging rightly?

IT IS EASY to persuade ourselves that our particular convictions are the standards of Christ, and to condemn every one who does not agree with us; we are obliged to do it because our convictions have taken the place of God in us. God's Book never tells us to walk in the light of convictions, but in the light of the Lord.^{SSM}

THE LIFE THAT steadily refuses to trust its own insight, is the only life that Satan cannot touch. Watch every time you get to a tight feeling spiritually, to a dry feeling rationally, to a hindered feeling physically, it is the Spirit of God's quiet warning that you should repair to the heavenly places in Christ Jesus. There is never any fear for the life that is hid with Christ in God, but there is not only fear, but terrible danger, for the life unguarded by God.[ITWBP]

Reflection Questions

What makes me agitated, anxious, and afraid? What might Satan be trying to keep me from doing? Where can I go to be safe?

THE GREAT OBJECT of the enemy of our souls is to make us fling away our confidence in God; to do this is nothing less than spiritual suicide. When we experience misgiving because we have sinned there is never any ambiguity as to its cause, the Holy Spirit brings conviction home like a lightning flash.[OPG]

In Despair: Hope *in the* SPIRIT

THE CONCEPTION OF faith given in the New Testament is that it must embrace the whole man. Faith is the whole man rightly related to God by the power of the Spirit of Jesus. We are apt to apply faith to certain domains of our lives only—we have faith in God when we ask Him to save us, or ask Him for the Holy Spirit, but we trust something other than God in the actual details of our lives. Our Lord lived His life not to show how good He was, but to put us into the relationship to God that He had.[CHI]

Reflection Questions
What domains of my life have I not
entrusted to God? Why?

WE CAN ALWAYS find a hundred and one reasons for not obeying our Lord's commands, because we will trust our reasoning rather than His reason, and our reason does not take God into calculation. How do we argue? "Does this man deserve what I am giving him?" Immediately you talk like that, the Spirit of God says, "Do *you* deserve more than other men the blessings you have?"[SSM]

IT APPEARS AS if God were sometimes most unnatural; we ask Him to bless our lives and bring benedictions, and what immediately follows turns everything into actual ruin. The reason is that before God can make the heart into a garden of the Lord, He has to plow it, and that will take away a great deal of natural beauty. If we interpret God's designs by our desires, we will say He gave us a stone when we asked for bread. But our Lord indicates that such thinking and speaking is too hasty, it is not born of faith or reliance on God.[CD]

Reflection Questions
In what areas have I judged God unfairly? Why? What made me think He was wrong?

THE HOLY SPIRIT not only brings us into the zone of God's influence but into intimate relationship with Him personally, so that by the slow discipline of prayer the choices of our free will become the preordinations of His Almighty order. When we say we have no faith, we simply betray our own case—that we have no confidence in God at all, for faith is born of confidence in Him.[CD]

In Despair: Hope *in the* SPIRIT

GOD'S WILL IS supreme, but God never fights against us; it is self-will that fights against God. When the Spirit of God is at work in him, a man lets God's will overcome, there is no fight, it is a higher power easily overcoming. If I view anything as inevitable with regard to any human being I am an unbeliever. I have no right to have anything less than the hope and the belief of Jesus Christ with regard to the worst and most hopeless of men.[NI]

Reflection Questions

What makes me think God is against me? Or against someone else? If God is only against those who are against Him, how can I make sure that I am on His side?

I ACCEPT HIM not only as my Authority, I accept Him as my Savior. I pin my faith implicitly to what He says; and looking to Him in implicit confidence, I ask God to give me the Holy Spirit according to the word of Jesus and receive Him in faith.[AUG]

WE ALL NEED someone who can make real to us the ideas we had of God but have forgotten; the only One who can do this for us is the Spirit of God. Isaiah brings back to the people first of all the memory of who God is; you cannot have faith in anyone you have forgotten. It is not God's promises we need, it is himself. "His presence is salvation." Once that Presence comes, all the inner forces of hope are rallied at once.[NI]

Reflection Questions

At Christmas we say, "God's presence is more important than presents." Do I really want His presence more than His presents? What gift of knowledge do I want more than God himself?

WHENEVER I SAY "I want to reason this thing out before I can trust," I will never trust. The perfection of knowledge comes after the response to God has been made. The whole of the New Testament exposition in the inspiration of the Holy Spirit is in order that we might know where we have been placed by Almighty God's Redemption.[GW]

In Despair: Hope *in the* SPIRIT

THINK OF THE worst man you know, not the worst man you can think of, for that is vague. Have you any hope for him? Does the Holy Spirit convey to you the wonder of that man being presented perfect in Christ Jesus? This test determines whether you are learning to think about men as Jesus thought of them. The Holy Spirit brings us into sympathy with the work Jesus has done on behalf of men in that He is "able to save them to the uttermost that come unto God by Him."[CHI]

Reflection Questions

In what ways do I limit God by thinking of certain people or situations as hopeless? What natural talents do I trust more than God?

THE GIFTS OF the Spirit are built on God's sovereignty, not on our temperament. What does it matter to the Lord Almighty what your early training was like! What matters to Him is that you don't lean on your own understanding, but acknowledge Him in all your ways. The great stumbling-block that prevents some people being simple disciples of Jesus is that they *are* gifted—so gifted that they won't trust in the Lord with all their hearts.[AUG]

THE TEST OF maturity is the power to look back without getting either hopelessly despairing or hopelessly conceited. Forgetting in the natural domain is the outcome of vanity—the only things I remember are those in which I figure as being a very fine person! Forgetting in the spiritual domain is the gift of God. The Spirit of God never allows us to forget what we have been, but He does make us forget what we have attained.^{CHI}

Reflection Questions

How much of my memory is based on what makes me look good? What would God have me remember or forget? How does memory affect hope?

SOME OF US have not allowed God to make us understand how hopeless we are without Jesus Christ. Everyone who is born again of the Spirit of God knows that there is no good thing outside the Lord Jesus Christ. It is no use looking for sanctification through prayer or obedience; sanctification must be the direct gift of God by means of this instrument of faith.^{OBH}

In Despair: Hope *in the* SPIRIT

GOD NEVER REVEALS himself in the same way to everyone, and yet the testimony of each one who has a revelation of God is the same—that God is love. Job's faith wavers under the blows of the providence of God and the stinging cruelty of his friends. From the delirium of his perplexity he pleads for pity. And then a new confidence seems to creep in; the Spirit of God begins to lift him to a higher plane; his consciousness of innocence is confirmed as God reveals himself in a more majestic and mysterious way.[GW]

Reflection Questions

Do I lose hope because I've not seen God work in me as He has in others? What has God done in me that He hasn't done in others? Would I rather have a one-of-a-kind encounter with God or a re-run of someone else's?

JOB HAS A growing assurance that he will yet be justified in the eyes of those who now accuse him, and he repeats to himself his confidence. The darkness is transformed by the never-to-be-explained rapture of his growing realization of God.[GW]

Peter tells us to be ready always to give an answer to everyone who asks us a reason concerning the hope that is in us. He did not say give reasonings, but a reason. We can give a reason for what we know, but we cannot reason it out with the man who has not the same spirit. We can state that we are right with God because we have received His Spirit on the word of Jesus, but our reasonings are nonsense to the man who has not accepted the Holy Spirit.^{ITWBP} [ITWBP]

Reflection Questions

Am I content to give a reason for my hope or do I insist that my reason should be enough for someone else? Why do I have so little patience with the work of the Holy Spirit in the life of others?

We wait in hope for the revelation of the Lord Jesus Christ. The Holy Ghost is seeking to awaken men out of lethargy; He is pleading, yearning, blessing, pouring benedictions on men, convicting and drawing them nearer, for one purpose only, that they may receive Him so that He may make them holy men and women exhibiting the life of Jesus Christ.[BE]

"DON'T BUILD YOUR hopes again on anything you can see; don't put your confidence again in men, in alliances with Egypt and Assyria; they all wither as the grass." Then comes the heartening verity—"but the word of our God shall stand for ever." Everything will shift but God and His word. How steadily the Spirit of God warns us not to put our trust in men and women, not even in princes, or in anything or anyone but God and His word."[NI]

Reflection Questions

In what ways do I ignore the warning of God's Spirit that I should not place my hope in anything material? What trouble am I inviting when I do?

SANCTIFICATION IS SAYING farewell once and for ever to having confidence in anyone but God. Then the hundred-fold can be given without any fear of deceiving the heart.[NI]

SPIRITUAL CLEVERNESS IS the cause of much of our failure. We may not have much mental cleverness, but some of us are dexterously clever spiritually. We have so many memories of the times when God came in and did the thing that we determinedly "loaf" on God—only we call it "relying on the Holy Ghost." There are times when God does give real spiritual insight and times when He does not, and if between the times of inspiration you do not work but "loaf," you are leading up to tremendous failure. NKW

Reflection Questions

How much of my "resting" in God is really spiritual "loafing"? What inspiration have I received that I have not yet put into action?

THE MOMENTS OF light and inspiration are an indication of the standard which we must work to keep up. If between the times of inspiration we refuse to practice, we shall fail spiritually exactly where others fail intellectually. They fail because they trust clever moments of their own genius, and we fail because we trust moments of spiritual cleverness. NKW

In Despair: Hope *in the* SPIRIT

LOOK BACK OVER your own history with God in prayer, and you will find that the glib days of prayer are done. When we draw on the human side of our experience only, our prayers become amazingly flippant and familiar, and we ourselves become amazingly hard and metallic; but if along with the human element we rely on the Holy Spirit, we shall find that our prayers become more and more inarticulate; and when they are inarticulate, reverence grows deeper and deeper, and undue familiarity has the effect of a sudden blow on the face.[IYSA]

Reflection Questions

Do my prayers sound more like a memorized script for an audience, a polite greeting to an acquaintance, or a heartfelt conversation with someone I love?

THERE IS SOMETHING hopelessly incongruous in a flippant statement before God. Am I growing slowly to lisp the very prayers of God? Is God gratified (if I may use the phrase) in seeing that His Spirit is having His way at last in a life, and turning that life into what will glorify His Son?[IYSA]

How MUCH FAITH, hope, and love is worked in us when we try to convince somebody else? It is not our business to convince other people, that is the insistence of a merely intellectual, unspiritual life. We exploit the word of God when we try to fit it into some view of our own that we have generated. The Spirit of God will do the convicting when we are in the relationship where we simply convey God's word.[ITWBP]

Reflection Questions

Am I content doing the work assigned to me—planting and watering seeds of hope—or do I also try to make them grow? Do I try to carry others to the side of faith, or do I wait for them to trust the Holy Spirit?

We PUT ONE foot on God's side and one on the side of human reasoning; then God widens the space and we either drop down or jump to one side or the other. We have to take a leap, and if we have learned to rely on the Holy Ghost, it will be a reckless leap to God's side. Many of us limit our praying because we are not reckless in our confidence in God.[IYSA]

In Despair: Hope in the SPIRIT

To BECOME "AS little children" means to receive a new heredity, a totally new nature, the essence of which is simplicity and confidence toward God. To develop the moral life, innocence must be transformed into virtue by a series of deliberate choices in which present pleasure is sacrificed for the ultimate joy of being good. We have no choice about being born into this world, but to be born again, to come to Jesus and receive His Spirit, is within our own power. Likewise, we can be renewed in the spirit of our minds whenever we choose.[BE]

Reflection Questions

Is my hope childlike or childish? Do I trust my heavenly Father to give me what I need, or do I nag to get what I want? Am I willing to receive what I don't want to have?

WHEN PEOPLE SAY, "Preach us the simple Gospel," they mean, "Preach us the thing we have always heard, the thing that keeps us sound asleep, we don't want to see things differently." Continual renewal of mind is the only healthy state for a Christian. Beware of the ban of finality about your present views.[BE]

WHEN WE ARE young in grace there is a note of independence about our spiritual life—an independence based on inexperience and lack of devotion. Some of us never get beyond it; but we are built for God, himself, not for service for God, and that explains the submissions of life. When we become disciples of Jesus we cannot remain independent. Jesus expects nothing less than absolute oneness with himself as He was one with the Father. That is the "hope of His calling" and it is the great light on every problem.AUG

Reflection Questions

What sacrifice do I need to make so that I can be made one with Christ and with other Christians? What hope for oneness in heaven do I have if I make no effort on earth?

THE HOPE OF *His* calling is that we are part of the glory of *His* inheritance. This unveils to our hearts an understanding of our Lord's great prayer "that they may be one, even as we are one." One in holiness, one in love, one for ever with God the Father, God the Son, and God the Holy Ghost.CD

In Despair: Hope *in the* SPIRIT

THE DEVIL IS a bully, but he cannot stand for a second before God. When we stand in the armor of God he pays no attention to us, but if we tackle the devil in our own strength we are done for. If we stand in God's armor with the strength and courage of God, he cannot gain one inch of way, and the position of prayer is held, untouched by his wiles. Confidence in the natural world is self-reliance, in the spiritual world it is God-reliance.[IYSA]

Reflection Questions

What piece of armor do I forget (or refuse) to wear—the belt of truth, the breastplate of righteousness, the gospel of peace, the shield of faith, the helmet of salvation, or the sword of the Spirit?

THE ONLY WAY to be prepared for the devil is to stand complete in God's armor, indwelt by His Spirit, in complete obedience to Him. The enemy is here all the time and he is wily. The secret of the sacred struggle is standing in the armor of God, practicing what God would have us do, then we can hold the position of prayer against all the attacks of the devil.[IYSA]

WHEN THE SPIRIT of God comes into a soul there is darkness and difficulty because this new disposition makes the spirit yearn and long after being made like God, and nothing and no one but God can comfort the soul that is born of the Spirit. The only hope for that life is concentration on and obedience to the Spirit of God.[BP]

Reflection Questions

What darkness and difficulty am I able to see more clearly since being led to faith in God?

What discouragement sets in because I now see so much hopelessness in those without God?

How can I keep from being discouraged?

THE CENTER OF life and of thinking for the Christian is the Person of Jesus Christ. We become "respectable" when we face only the problems we have been used to facing; but if we obey the Holy Spirit He will bring us to face other problems, and as we face them through personal relationship to Jesus Christ we shall go forth with courage, confident that no situation worries Him.[GW]

In Despair: Hope *in the* SPIRIT

IF I SAY, "God would never convey a right interpretation of himself through a handful of men like the disciples," I am casting a slur on what Jesus said, telling Him that His reliance on God's promise of the Spirit was without justification; that His basis of confidence on the Holy Spirit's revelation of himself to the disciples was misplaced. When our Lord told the disciples they would do "greater works," His reliance was not on them, but on the gift of the Spirit which He was to receive from the Father and shed forth on them. Everything Jesus said the Holy Spirit would do, He has done and the New Testament is the revelation of it.[CHI]

Reflection Questions
What do I think God could accomplish through the disciples that He cannot accomplish through me?

IF WE TRY to fight God's battles with our own weapons, in our own moral resisting power, we shall fail, and fail miserably; but if we use the spiritual weapons of implicitly trusting in God and maintaining a simple relationship to Jesus Christ by praying in the Holy Ghost, we shall never fail.[LG]

IF WE WILL let the Spirit of God bring us face to face with God we too shall hear something akin to what Isaiah heard, the still, small voice of God, and in perfect freedom say, "Here am I; send me." We have to get out of our minds the idea of expecting God to come with compulsion and pleadings. When Our Lord called His disciples there was no irresistible compulsion from outside; the quiet, passionate insistence of His "Follow Me" was spoken to men with every power wide awake.[NI]

---

*R*eflection *Q*uestions

Am I waiting to hear God say something other than "follow Me"? Am I expecting Him to give me something before I say, "Here I am, send me"?

IN THE EYES of those who do not know God, it is madness to trust Him, but when we pray in the Holy Ghost we begin to realize the resources of God, that He is our perfect heavenly Father, and we are His children.[IYSA]

WILL I BE absolutely confident in Jesus? What does it matter what happens to me? The thought ought never to bother us, the thing that ought to occupy us is setting the Lord always before us (cf. Acts 20:24). Jesus Christ imparts the Holy Spirit to me, and the Holy Spirit sheds abroad the love of God in my heart (see Rom. 5:5). The peace of Jesus is not a cherished piece of property that I possess; it is a direct impartation from Him, and my enjoying His peace depends on my recognizing this.[CD]

Reflection Questions

Do I try to possess peace as if it were property? Or do I act as a conduit of peace so that it can flow from God through me to others?

IT IS NOT only necessary to have an experience of God's grace, we must have a body of beliefs alive with the Spirit of Jesus, then when we have learned to see men as He sees them, there is no form of disease or anguish or devilishness that can disturb our confidence in Him; if it does disturb us, it is because we don't know Him.[HG]

AGREEMENT IN PURPOSE on earth must not be taken to mean a predetermination to agree together to storm God's fort doggedly till He yields. It is far from right to agree beforehand over what we want, and then go to God and wait, not until He gives us His mind about the matter, but until we extort from Him permission to do what we had made up our minds to do before we prayed; we should rather agree to ask God to convey His mind and meaning to us in regard to the matter.[CD]

Reflection Questions

Is my hope in God based on my ability to get from Him what I want or on God's ability to give me what I need?

AGREEMENT IN PURPOSE on earth is not a public presentation of persistent begging which knows no limit, but a prayer which is conscious that it is limited through the moral nature of the Holy Ghost. It is really "symphonizing" on earth with our Father Who is in heaven.[CD]

FAITH, HOPE, LOVE, the three supernatural virtues, have a two-fold aspect in the saint's life. The first is seen in the early experiences of grace when these virtues are accidental; the second, when grace is worked into us and these virtues are essential and abiding. When the work of God's grace begins, "the love of God is shed abroad in our hearts by the Holy Ghost," not the power to love God, but the essential nature of God.[ITWBP]

Reflection Questions

Are the virtues of faith, hope, and love accidental, essential, or abiding in me? In what ways is God's presence in me crowding out the "no good things" that have been living there comfortably?

JESUS NEVER TRUSTED any man whether it was John, or Peter, or Thomas; He knew what was in them: they did not. The Holy Spirit applies Jesus Christ's knowledge to me until I know that "in me, that is, in my flesh, dwells no good thing." Consequently I am never dismayed at what I discover in myself, but learn to trust only what the grace of God does in me.[CHI]

THE ATTITUDE OF those not indwelled by the Spirit of God is that man's abilities are a promise of what he is going to be: the Holy Ghost sees man as a ruin of what he once was. He does not delight in our natural virtues. When the Holy Ghost is having His way with us, the first thing He does is to corrupt confidence in virtues. Nothing is more highly esteemed among men than pride in my virtues, but Jesus said, "that which is highly esteemed among men is abomination in the sight of God."[CHI]

Reflection Questions

How much of the good I do is done in the strength of my own virtue rather than the power of the Holy Spirit? Does this result in pride or humility?

WHEN YOU ARE in such a relationship to God that you do good without knowing you do it, then you will no longer trust your own impulse or judgment, you will trust only the inspiration of the Spirit of God. The mainspring of your motives will be the Father's heart, not your own; the Father's understanding, not your own. When you are rightly related to God, He will use you as a channel through which His disposition will flow.[SSM]

In Despair: Hope in the SPIRIT

WHEN LIFE IS twisted, we are in the state of heart and mind to understand why it was necessary for God to become Incarnate. The doctrine of the Self-limitation of Jesus is clear to our hearts first, not to our heads. We cannot form the mind of Christ unless we have His Spirit; once we receive His Spirit we know implicitly what He means. Things which to the intellect may be hopelessly bewildering are lustrously clear to the heart of the humble saint.[MFL]

Reflection Questions

Am I hoping to have the mind of Christ without first having His Spirit? Why is it impossible to know God's mind without first understanding His heart?

WHEN THROUGH JESUS Christ we are rightly related to God, we learn to watch and wait, and wait wonderingly. "I wonder how God will answer this prayer." "I wonder how God will answer the prayer the Holy Ghost is praying in me." "I wonder what glory God will bring to Himself out of the strange perplexities I am in." "I wonder what new turn His providence will take in manifesting Himself in my ways."[IYSA]

THE TRUE NATURE of a man's heart is that of expectation and hope. It is the heart that is strengthened by God (cf. Psalm 73:26), and Jesus Christ said that He came to "bind up the broken hearted." The marvel of the indwelling Spirit of God is that He can give heart to a despairing man.[MFL]

Reflection Questions

What more do I hope to receive from God than sympathy? How does God's hope for me transcend sympathy? Why would I settle for sympathy when I can have restoration?

THERE IS A difference between the human sympathy we give to a discouraged man and what the Holy Spirit will do for him. We may sit down beside a broken-hearted man and pour out a flow of sympathy, and say how sorry we are for him, and tell him of other people with broken hearts; but all that only makes him more submissive to being broken-hearted. When our Lord sympathizes with the heart broken by sin or sorrow, He binds it up and makes it a new heart, and the expectation of that heart ever after is from God.[MFL]

In Despair: Hope *in the* SPIRIT

THE WORK OF the Spirit of God in us transcends reason, but never contradicts it, and when a Christian says "the reason I am so-and-so is because I have received the Holy Spirit," or, "I have received from God something which has made this possible," it does not contradict reason, it transcends it, and is an answer concerning the hope that is in you. The line we are continually apt to be caught by is that of argumentative reasoning out why we are what we are; we can never do that, but we can always say why the hope is in us.^{GW}

Reflection Questions

Does my hope more often involve arguments about what I believe or actions expressing what I know? Which is better? Why?

THERE IS NOT a saint among us who can give explicit reasons concerning the hope that is in us, but we can always give this reason: we have received the Holy Spirit, and He has witnessed that the truths of Jesus are the truth.^{ITWBP}

THE MAN WITHOUT the Spirit of God has no power of perception, he cannot perceive God's working behind ordinary occurrences. The events of ordinary days and nights present facts we cannot explain, the only way to explain them is by receiving the Spirit of God Who will impart to us an interpretation that will keep the heart strong and confident in God, because it gives us an understanding of God Who is behind all things.[TWBP]

Reflection Questions

What facts am I trying to explain apart from the interpretation of the Holy Spirit? What virtues am I trying to attain apart from the indwelling of the Holy Spirit?

WHEN WE EXPERIENCE what we call being born again of the Spirit of God, we have "spurts" of faith, hope, love; they come but we cannot grip them and they go; when we experience what we call sanctification, those virtues abide, they are not accidental any more. It is only by realizing the love of God in us by His grace that we are led by His entrancing power in us.[TWBP]

In Disaster

Hope *in* Jesus

IF A MAN will commit his "yesterday" to God, make it irrevocable, and bank in confidence on what Jesus Christ has done, his mouth will be filled with laughter, and his tongue with singing. Very few of us get there because we do not believe Jesus Christ means what He says. Can Jesus Christ re-make me, with my meanness and my criminality; re-make my mind and my dreams?" Jesus said, "With God all things are possible." The reason God cannot do it for us is because of our unbelief; it is not that God *won't* do it if we do not believe, but that our commitment to Him is part of the essential relationship.PH

Reflection Questions

What am I missing because I refuse to believe in the hope God has for me?

THE ACCUSER OF the brethren says to God, "That man is a broken reed, don't build any hope on him whatever, he is a hindrance and an upset to You; break him." But no, the Lord will bind up the broken reed and make it into a wonderful instrument and discourse sweet music through it.NI

In Disaster: Hope *in* JESUS

IF ANYTHING WE may be told about God contradicts the manifestation given by Jesus Christ, we are at liberty to say, "No, I cannot believe that." Things have been taught about God which are seen to be diabolical when viewed in the light of Our Lord's revelation of Him. Remain steadfastly true to what you have learned, and when you have to suspend your judgment, say it is suspended. This was Job's attitude all through. "Your creed distorts the character of God, but I know in the end He will prove to be all that I trust Him to be, a God of love and justice, and absolutely honorable."[BFB]

Reflection Questions

What belief am I unwilling to give up even though God never said it is true? Why are certain beliefs more comforting to me than actual truth?

WE SENTIMENTALLY BELIEVE, and believe, and believe, and nothing happens. We try to pump up our faith, but it does not come. What is wrong? The moral surrender has not taken place. Will I surrender from the real center of my life, and deliberately and willfully stake my confidence on what Jesus Christ tells me?[AUG]

A SPIRITUALLY MINDED Christian has to go through the throes of a total mental readjustment; it is a God-glorifying process, if a humbling one. People continually say, "How can I have more faith?" You will never have faith apart from Jesus Christ. You can't pump up faith out of your own heart. Whenever faith is starved in your soul it is because you are not in contact with Jesus. The only ones who were without faith in Him were those who were bound up by religious certitude. Faith means that I commit myself to Jesus. Faith is implicit confidence in Jesus and in His faith.[CHI]

Reflection Questions

In what circumstances do I put my religious convictions ahead of Christ? What hope does Jesus have that I don't have? Why don't I have it?

IS JESUS CHRIST a Carpenter, or is He God to me? If He is only man, why let Him take the tiller of the boat? Why pray to Him? But if He be God, then be heroic enough to go to the breaking-point and not break in your confidence in Him.[PH]

In Disaster: Hope *in* JESUS

BEFORE YOU SEAL your opinion on any matter, find out what Jesus has said about it—about God, about life, about death. Men discuss matters of heaven and hell, of life and death, and leave Jesus Christ out altogether; He says, "Before you finally seal your mind, Believe *also* in Me." If the bit we do know about Jesus Christ is so full of light, why cannot we leave the matters of heaven and hell, of life and death, in His hand and stake our confidence in Him? "God is light," and one day everything will be seen in that light. Theology ought to be discussed; it does not follow, however, that our faith is assailed, but that in the meantime we stake our all in Jesus Christ.[AUG]

Reflection Questions

Which topics of discussion do I not invite Jesus to join? What makes me afraid of hearing what He has to say? What can I possibly gain by trusting what I think rather than what He knows?

CHRISTIAN FAITH MEANS putting our confidence in the efficacy of Christ's work.[PH]

THERE IS NO joy in a personality unless it can create. The joy of an artist is not in the fame which his pictures bring him, but that his work is the creation of his personality. The work of Jesus is the creation of saints; He can take the worst, the most misshapen material, and make a saint. That is, He creates in us what He is himself. The apostle Paul alludes to the joy of creating when he says, "For what is our hope, or joy, or crown of rejoicing? Is it not even you . . . ? For you are our glory and our joy" (1 Thess. 2:19–20).[BSG]

*R*eflection *Q*uestions
If I believe that God created the universe out of nothing, why do I resist what He wants to create in and through me?

FAITH MEANS IMPLICIT confidence in Jesus, and that requires not intellect only but a moral giving over of myself to Him, to the Spirit that ruled Jesus Christ and kept His spirit, soul and body in harmony with God.[AUG]

In Disaster: Hope *in* JESUS

WHEN JESUS MET a man who could sink to the level of Judas He never turned cynical, lost heart, or got discouraged; and when He met a loyal loving heart like John's, He was not unduly elated. When we meet extra goodness we feel hopeful about everybody, and when we meet extra badness we feel exactly the opposite; but Jesus knew exactly what human beings were like and what they needed; and He saw in them something no one else ever saw—hope for the most degraded. Jesus had a tremendous hopefulness about man.^{CHI}

Reflection Questions

Do I have hope that Jesus can exalt the lowest of all people? Do I have confidence that He will bring down those who have exalted themselves?

IF JESUS IS not revealed to us it is because we want to bend everything to our own views. To realize Christ we must trust Someone other than ourselves; to do this we must deliberately efface ourselves. Devotion and piety are opponents of Jesus Christ when we devote ourselves to devotion instead of to Him.^{PR}

IN THE BEGINNING Philip obeyed Jesus Christ readily, there was no traitorous unbelief in his heart; he realized who Jesus was, and testified of Him to others, and yet he did not have perfect childlike confidence in Jesus. If you know only what you have experienced, you will never see Jesus. You can never rely on what you believe intellectually; but once have the attitude of a perfectly simple, unsophisticated child of God and there is no trouble in believing.^{GW} [GW]

Reflection Questions

How much of my time do I spend trying to "collect" experiences with God as opposed to simply spending time with Him?

IN THE MYSTICAL life the majority of us are hopeless wool gatherers, we have never learned to brood on such subjects as "abiding in Christ." We have to form the habit of abiding until we come into the relationship with God where we rely upon Him almost unconsciously in every particular.[MFL]

IS YOUR MIND set on Jesus Christ, or have you only a principle at stake? The great simplicity of the Christian life is the relationship to the Highest. Reckless confidence in God is of far more value than personal holiness, if personal holiness is looked upon as an end in itself. When once you take any one of the great works of God as an end, or any one of the truths which depend on Jesus Christ, as *the* truth, you will go wrong, you are outside the guard of God. The safeguard is the Highest—"I am . . . the Truth." "I, if I be lifted up . . ." Allow nothing to take you away from Jesus himself, and all other phases of truth will take their right place.^{GW}

Reflection Questions

Do I consider holiness as something to achieve so that I can be rightly related to God or as something that I receive as a result of being in the right relationship with God?

"THE BEST IS yet to be" is really true from Jesus Christ's standpoint. There is nothing noble the human mind has ever hoped for or dreamed of that will not be fulfilled, and a great deal more.^{HSGM}

To be a believer does not mean that we believe Jesus Christ can *do* things, or that we believe in a plan of salvation; it is that we believe *Him;* whatever happens we will hang on to the fact that He is true. If we say, "I believe He will put things right," we shall lose our confidence when we see things go wrong. We put the cart before the horse in saying that a man must believe certain things before he can be a Christian; beliefs are the result of being a Christian, not the cause.[AUG]

Reflection Questions

In what circumstances has my hope been shaken because I was trusting in my own convictions rather than in Christ?

Immorality has its seat in every one of us, not in some of us. If a man is not holy, he is immoral, no matter how good he may seem. Immorality is at the basis of the whole thing; if it does not show itself outwardly, it will show itself before God. Never trust your common sense when the statements of Jesus contradict it.[AUG]

IT IS NOT our earnestness that brings us into touch with God, nor our devotedness, nor our times of prayer, but our Lord Jesus Christ's vitalizing death; and our times of prayer are evidences of reaction on the reality of Redemption, so we have confidence and boldness of access into the holiest. What an unspeakable joy it is to know that we each have the right of approach to God in confidence, that the place of the Ark is our place, "Having therefore, brethren, boldness." What an awe and what a wonder of privilege, "to enter into the holiest," in the perfectness of the Atonement, "by the blood of Jesus."[CD]

Reflection Questions
What fear or false hope keeps me from following Jesus unreservedly?

NEITHER FEAR OF hell nor hope of heaven has anything to do with our personal relationship to Jesus Christ, it is a life hid with Christ in God, stripped of all possessions saving the knowledge of Him. The great lodestar of the life is Jesus Himself, not anything He does for us.[MFL]

LET A MAN be a murderer, or an evildoer, or any of the things Jesus said men could be, it can never shake our confidence if we have once been face to face with Jesus Christ for ourselves. It is impossible to discourage us because we start from a knowledge of Who Jesus Christ is in our own life. When we see evil and wrong exhibited in other lives, instead of awakening a sickening despair, it awakens a joyful confidence—I know a Savior who can save even that one.[HG]

Reflection Questions

How do I respond to evil in the world—with resigned hopelessness or joyful confidence? Do I consider evil a warning from Satan to retreat or a call from God to advance?

THE NEW TESTAMENT conception of heaven is "hereafter" without the sin, "new heavens and a new earth, wherein dwells righteousness"—a conception beyond us. An undefiled inheritance awaits us, and in it is all we have ever hoped or dreamed or imagined, and a good deal more. It is always *Better to come* in the Christian life until the *Best of all* comes.[PH]

In Disaster: Hope *in* JESUS

MANY A ONE who has started the imitation of Christ has had to abandon it as hopeless because a strain is put on human nature that human nature cannot begin to live up to. To have attitudes of life without the life itself is a fraud. The teaching of Jesus Christ applies only to the life He puts in, and the marvel of His Redemption is that He gives the power of His own disposition to carry any man through who is willing to obey Him.[AUG]

Reflection Questions

What danger to me are my "natural" virtues? How do they hinder my hope? How do they block my walk with Jesus?

NEVER TAKE ANYONE to be good, and above all never take yourself to be good. Natural goodness will always break, always disappoint, why? Because "the heart is deceitful above all things, and desperately wicked: who can know it?" Never trust anything in yourself that God has not placed there through the regeneration of Our Lord Jesus Christ.[AUG]

NO AMOUNT OF sacrifice on the part of man can put the basis of human life right: God has undertaken the responsibility for this, and He does it on redemptive lines. Imagine a man seeing hell without at the same time perceiving salvation through Jesus Christ—his reason must totter. Pseudo-evangelism makes an enormous blunder when it insists on conviction of sin as the first step to Jesus Christ. When we have come to the place of seeing Jesus Christ, then He can trust us with the facing of sin.[BFB]

Reflection Questions

Why is it important for people to see Jesus before facing their sin? How can anyone recognize hopelessness without first seeing hope?

OUR FAITH IS in a Person Who is not deceived in anything He says or in the way He looks at things. Christianity is personal, passionate devotion to Jesus Christ as God manifest in the flesh.[AUG]

In Disaster: Hope *in* JESUS

OUR FATHER GATHERS us near Him in the secret place alone with our fears and apprehensions and foolishnesses and aspirations, and He rewards us. When we talk about the Fatherhood of God, let us remember that the Lord Jesus is the exclusive way to the Father. That is not an idea to be inferred, but to be received: "No man comes to the Father, but by Me" (John 14:6). We can get to God as Creator apart from Jesus Christ (Rom. 1:20), but never to God as our Father except through Him. Let us receive this inspired idea of our Lord's right into our inmost willing heart, believe it, and pray in the confidence of it.[CD]

Reflection Questions

What evidence do I see in myself that the life of Jesus is being formed in me?

HAVE WE THE quiet confidence of a child that the life of Jesus Christ can be formed in us until the relationship to God of spirit, soul, and body is without blame before Him? It is not the perfection of attainment in thinking, or in bodily life, or in worship, but the perfection of a blameless disposition, nothing in it to censure, and that in the eyes of God who sees everything.[LG]

OUR LIFE IS drawn from the Lord Jesus, not only the spring and the motive of the life, but our actual thinking and living and doing. Notice how God will wither up every other spring you have. He will wither up your natural virtues, He will break up confidence in your natural powers, He will wither up your confidence in brain and spirit and body, until you learn by practical experience that you have no right to draw your life from any source other than the tremendous reservoir of the resurrection life of Jesus Christ.[BP]

Reflection Questions

From what source other than God do I draw strength—family, friends, resources, intelligence, personality, talent? Why will these ultimately lead to despair?

TO THINK FAIR and square is not to see goodness and purity everywhere, but to see something that produces despair. When a man sees life as it really is there are only two alternatives—the Cross of Jesus Christ as something to accept, or suicide. We are shielded by a merciful density, by a curious temperament of hopefulness that keeps us blind to the desolating desert.[HSGM]

HAVE WE EVER caught the full force of the thirty silent years, of those three years wandering in Palestine? Have we ever caught the full force of those ten days of waiting in the upper room? If we measure those periods by our modern way of estimating we will put it down as waste of time; but into the life of Our Lord, and into the lives of the early disciples, were going to come elements that would root and ground them on a solid foundation that nothing could shake. The waiting time is always the testing time. How we hurry people into work for God! Picture those silent years in the life of Our Lord, shielded by His Father, until all the tremendous forces of His life were developed and grasped.[BSG]

Reflection Questions

What makes me impatient with God?

Why am I afraid of waiting and resting?

THE ONLY HOPE for a man lies not in giving him an example of how to behave, but in the preaching of Jesus Christ as the Savior from *sin.* The heart of every man gets hope when he hears that.[DI]

REFUSE TO BE swamped by the cares of this world.
Cut out nonessentials and continually revise your relationship to God and concentrate absolutely on Him.
The one who trusts Christ in a definite practical way is
freer than anyone else to do His work. Free from fret
and worry, he can go with absolute certainty into daily
life because the responsibility is not on him but on God.
When we accept the revelation of Jesus that God is our
Father, and that we can never think of anything He will
forget, worry becomes impossible.^{SSM}

Reflection Questions

*What burdens have I picked up that Jesus
doesn't want me to carry? What problem am I
trying to explain that is not yet meant
for me to understand?*

THE MAJORITY OF us only believe in Jesus as far as
we can see. If we really believed Him, we would trust
His Mind instead of our own; we would stop being "am-
ateur providences" over other lives; we would be fit to
do our twenty-four hours' work like no one else; and
we would be as little children, simple-hearted, trusting,
and unafraid.^{BE}

In Disaster: Hope *in* JESUS

IF I TRUST Jesus Christ's diagnosis and hand over the keeping of my heart to Him, I need never experience personal depravity, but if I don't, I am likely to one day turn a corner and find that what He said is true. When the crisis comes and men find that what they took to be their innocent heart is really a sink of iniquity, they would be the first to say, "Why did not God tell us?" "Why were we not warned?" We are warned, perfectly clearly, in order that we need never go through the terrible experience of knowing the truth of what Jesus said—"For from within, out of the heart of men, evil thoughts proceed . . ."—that is the marvelous mercy of God. Jesus Christ's teaching never beats about the bush. Our stupidity is to believe only what we are conscious of and not the revelation He has made.^{OPG}

Reflection Questions

What depravity could I have avoided if I had simply believed and trusted what Jesus said?

THE IMPORTANT THING to remember is that we are better trusting the revelations of Jesus Christ than our own innocence.^{OPG}

THE GREAT NOTE of the Bible revelation is not immortality but Resurrection. The doctrine of the Resurrection is that something comes from God himself direct into the dust of death. Dust is the symbol of death. A dead body retains the look of life, but touch it, and it is gone. The Resurrection is the manifestation of the direct power of God, not the manifestation of inherent life. The Bible always goes back to God; books go into vague hopes that cannot be realized in this life. Christianity is centered in the power of God, and the resurrection is the direct work of the sovereign God. When the apostle Paul wants to measure the power of God in our lives he uses the illustration of the resurrection of Jesus Christ from the dead (Rom. 8:11; Eph. 1:19–20).[NI]

Reflection Questions

Why does my hope depend on the resurrection of Jesus? In what way is the resurrected Christ living through me?

WILL I TRUST the revelation given of God by Jesus Christ when everything in my personal experience flatly contradicts it?[BFB]

SUPPOSING THERE WAS a certain region of earth about which you knew nothing and you received a communication from someone who said "I have never been to the country but this map is a sure guide"; and you also received a communication from someone who sent you no map but who said, "I have been to this country myself and if you will trust yourself to me I will guide you straight there"; how absurd it would be to trust to the information which was not firsthand and not go with the one who had been there and knew the way.[HSGM]

Reflection Questions
If I want to get to heaven,
why would I place my hope in anyone
(or anything) but Jesus?

SCRIPTURAL FAITH IS not to be illustrated by the faith we exhibit in our commonsense life, it is trust in the character of One we have never seen, in the integrity of Jesus Christ, and it must be tried.[PH]

THE ONE GREAT challenge is—Do I know my risen Lord? Do I know the power of His indwelling Spirit? Am I wise enough in God's sight, and foolish enough according to the world, to bank on what Jesus Christ has said; or am I abandoning the great supernatural position, which is boundless confidence in Christ Jesus? If I take up any other method, I depart altogether from the method laid down by Our Lord.^{CG}

Reflection Questions

What evidence can I see that Jesus is living in me? What crisis has come that He has guided me through?

WHEN WE BELIEVE *in* Jesus Christ, not *about* Him, it is evidence that God is at work in our souls. If we believe in a state of mind He produces in us, we will be disappointed, because circumstances will come in our lives when these works of Jesus Christ are shadowed over; but if we believe in Him, no matter how dark the passage is, we shall be carried right through, and when the crisis is passed our souls will have been built up into a stronger attitude towards Him.^{AUG}

In Disaster: Hope *in* JESUS

ONE GREAT HINDRANCE of our spiritual life lies in looking for big things to do. We are meant to be the common stuff of ordinary human life exhibiting the marvel of the grace of God. The snare in Christian life is in looking for the gilt-edged moments, the thrilling times; there are times when there is no illumination and no thrill, when God's routine for us involves towels and washing feet. Routine is God's way of saving us between our times of inspiration. We are not to expect Him to always give us thrilling minutes.[OBH]

Reflection Questions
What unrealistic expectations do I have? In what ways do I demonstrate my willingness to do "small" things for God?

THE LIFE OF Jesus is a wonderful example of a perfect human life, but what is the good of presenting to us spotless holiness that we are hopeless to attain? The revelation made by the Redemption is that God can put into us a new disposition whereby we can live a totally new life.[PR]

YOUR LIFE IS never safeguarded until Jesus is seen to be the Highest. Past experience will not keep you, neither will deliverance from sin; the only safeguarding power is the Highest. If there is a breath of confidence anywhere else, there will be disaster, and it is by the mercy of God that you are allowed to stumble, or be pain-smitten, until you learn that He does it all—He keeps you from stumbling, He raises you up and keeps you up, *He* sends from above and delivers you.^{GW} [GW]

Reflection Questions

What causes me to stumble and fall? Will I allow it to keep me down or will I allow Jesus to pick me up?

THE LORD JESUS Christ is the one Person to Whom we ought to yield, and we must be perfectly certain that it is to himself that we are yielding. Do not be sorry if other appeals find you stiff-necked and unyielding; but be sorry if, when He says "Come unto Me," you do not come. The attitude of coming is that the will resolutely lets go of everything and deliberately commits all to Him.[PR]

In Disaster: Hope *in* JESUS

THE MAJORITY OF us start out with the belief that God is good and kind, and that He prospers those who trust in Him. Job believed this, but he had a conscious resurgence against that belief, and it is Job's goodness, not his badness, which made him reconsider things. There are experiences which call for a revision of our credal findings about God.[BFB]

Reflection Questions

What creeds am I allowing to keep me separated from Christ? What problems am I allowing to compromise God's promises?

THE PROBLEMS OF life get hold of a man and make it difficult for him to know whether in the face of things like war and disease he really is confident in Jesus Christ. The attitude of a believer must be, "Things do look black, but I believe Him; and when the whole thing is told I am confident my belief will be justified and God will be revealed as a God of love and justice." It does not mean that we won't have problems, but it does mean that our problems will never come between us and our faith in Him.[AUG]

THE REALIZATION THAT my strength is a hindrance to God's supply of life is a great eye-opener. A man who has genius is apt to rely on his genius rather than on God. A man who has money is apt to rely on money instead of God. So many of us trust in what we have got in the way of possessions instead of entirely in God. All these sources of strength are sources of double weakness. Once we realize that our true life is "hid with Christ in God," that we are "complete in Him," in whom "dwells all the fullness of the Godhead bodily," then His strength is radiantly manifested in our mortal flesh.^{GW}

Reflection Questions

In what ways am I trusting God's gifts rather than God himself? What might God have me do that is outside my area of strength?

THE GREAT STUMBLING block in the way of some people being simple disciples is that they are gifted, so gifted that they won't trust God. So clear away all those things from the thought of discipleship; we all have absolutely equal privileges, and there is no limit to what God can do in and through us.^{ITWBP}

In Disaster: Hope *in* JESUS

ONE OF THE great words of God in our spiritual cal-
endar is NOW. It is not that we gradually get to God, or
gradually get away from Him; we are either there now or
we are not. We may get in touch with God not because
of our merit, but simply on the ground of the Redemption; and if any man has got out of touch with God in
the tiniest degree he can get back now, not presently;
not by trying to recall things that will exonerate him for
what he has done, but by an unconditional abandon to
Jesus Christ, and he will realize the efficacious power of
the resurrected Lord *now.* HSGM

Reflection Questions
*In what ways have I lost hope? What do I need
to do now to reaffirm my hope in Christ?*

VERY FEW OF us come to realize what is ours through
the resurrected Lord—that we can really draw on Him
for body, soul, and spirit now. We do not trust in a Christ
who died and rose again twenty centuries ago; He must
be a present Reality, an efficacious power now. HSGM

WE MAY HAVE to face destitution in order to maintain our spiritual connection with Jesus, and we can only do that if we love Him supremely. Every now and again there is the "last bridge"—"I have gone far enough, I can't go any further." If you are going on with God it is impossible to secure your interests at all. We have to go on in perfect confidence that our Father in heaven knows all about us.^{SHL}

Reflection Questions

What road seems impassable? What bridge do I not want to cross? What possible advantage would there be in staying where I am?

THERE IS NOTHING, naturally speaking, that makes us lose heart quicker than decay—the decay of bodily beauty, of natural life, of friendship, of associations, all these things make a man lose heart; but Paul says when we are trusting in Jesus Christ these things do not find us discouraged, light comes through them.^{PH}

AFTER SANCTIFICATION, GOD will wither up every other spring until we know that all our fresh springs are in Him. He will wither up natural virtues; He will break up all confidence in our own powers, until we learn by practical experience that we have no right to draw our life from any other source than the tremendous reservoir of the unsearchable riches of Jesus Christ.[OBH]

Reflection Questions

What personal power do I rely on?
What feelings or personal piety do I rely on?
What unsearchable riches of Christ should I rely on instead?

THE DANGER OF pietistic movements is that we are told what we must feel, and we can't get near God because we are so hopelessly dependent on pious attitudes.[DI]

WE ALL HAVE faith in good principles, in good management, in good common sense, but who among us has faith in Jesus Christ? Physical courage is grand, moral courage is grander, but the man who trusts Jesus Christ in the face of the terrific problems of life is worth a whole crowd of heroes.[HG]

Reflection Questions

How does my hope in Jesus transcend my confidence in such things as virtue and courage and practical principles of life in general?

THE FURTHER WE get away from Jesus the more dogmatic we become over what we call our religious beliefs, while the nearer we live to Jesus the less we have of certitude and the more of confidence in Him.[DI]

Index of Selections

Note to the Reader

The publisher invites you to share your response to the message of this book by writing Discovery House Publishers, P.O. Box 3566, Grand Rapids, MI 49501, U.S.A. or by calling 1-800-653-8333. For information about other Discovery House publications, contact us at the same address and phone number.